Understanding Sexuality

Belinda Tobin

UP

UNDERSTANDING PRESS

Understanding Sexuality

Copyright © 2024 by Belinda Tobin

Published by Understanding Press

UP

Paperback ISBN: 978-1-7637246-3-1
E-Book ISBN: 978-1-7637246-4-8
For permissions or enquiries, please contact:
Understanding Press
Email: up@heart-led.pub
Website: www.heart-led.pub/understanding-press
First Edition: October 2024

NATIONAL
LIBRARY
OF AUSTRALIA

A catalogue record for this
book is available from the
National Library of Australia

Other titles in The Understanding Series:
Understanding Violence
Understanding Monogamy
Understanding Addiction
Understanding Creativity

I acknowledge the Yuggera and Ugarapul peoples as the Traditional Owners of the lands and waterways where this book was written. I honour the wisdom that lives within the cultures of our First Nations peoples and celebrate its continuity. I pay my deep respects to Elders past, present and future and send my greatest gratitude for all they do for the life of this land.

Always was, always will be.

Contents

An Important Note

Please do not use this book as a substitute for expert advice or use the information contained within to disregard or delay seeking professional medical guidance. While proven models and relevant research are presented, this book does not contain a comprehensive scientific view of sexuality, and it is certainly not tailored to your specific context. Your personal environment and experiences are valuable and unique, and this book should be treated as a general guide only.

If you need to work through issues regarding your sexuality, please engage the assistance of a qualified therapist or counsellor. These professionals will not only help you address the questions arising for you now, but also empower you with vital self-awareness, communication and compassion skills that will serve you in good stead in the future.

Seeking help regarding your sexuality is not a sign of weakness. It is the greatest act of love, care, and respect for yourself and those around you.

Introduction

*"Sexuality is one of the ways that we become enlightened,
actually, because it leads us to self-knowledge."*
~ Alice Walker

I have heard sexuality described as a superpower, and I would agree that our sexuality does have amazing abilities. It has the potential to bring forth life and love, both within ourselves and with the world around us. We all exist because of a sexual union. So, at the core, our sexuality is a power of creation. It seeks to tap into the life force within us, to connect with the energies in the environment, and use this connection to make something valuable and unique. Our sexuality is a power that springs from the spirit we have inside of ourselves and seeks to share this life-creating energy with the world. In this way, I see our sexuality as the fundamental energy that drives creation at all levels, within ourselves, in communion with nature and connection with others.

The potency of our sexual power is evidenced by how much effort has been applied throughout history to suppress it. From Ancient Greece to the Victorian era, and across medieval Europe to colonial America, strict controls have been placed on human sexuality, often portraying it as a threat to social order or moral purity. Witch hunts, Puritanism, and the repression of the Victorian age exemplify how sexuality, especially women's, was stigmatised or criminalised.

Homosexuality, adultery, premarital sex, and expressions of sexuality were met with public humiliation, fines, and sometimes imprisonment. Men were imprisoned for sodomy or gross indecency (take Oscar Wilde, for example), and women were institutionalised for excess desires, also known as hysteria. In a practice that was tantamount to torture, children had their genitals sewn to prevent self-pleasure. Totalitarian regimes in the 20th Century further confined sexuality to roles of duty and reproduction, with sexuality to be used solely for the benefit of the State. Even today, certain religious and cultural norms continue to seek control over what a person's sexuality should be, and how it should be expressed. History has shown that there is both an enduring fascination, but also fear with the inherent human power of sexuality. As a result, it has been mangled by man's moral codes and laws, which leave a legacy of our sexuality as something evil and filthy.

"Sexuality must be daemonic if it requires such elaborate cultural work to contain it." ~ Adam Phillips[1]

However, while fear and repression were characteristic of Western cultures, Eastern philosophies have a vastly different approach to sexuality and provide a positive alternative, based on respect and compassion. For example, Tantric Buddhism seeks to mindfully channel sexual energy to facilitate spiritual transformation and the unification of opposing energies (often symbolized as masculine and feminine). In Hindu Tantra, sexual rituals are sometimes used as a means of experiencing oneness in both a physical and spiritual sense. In Taoism, particularly within practices of Taoist Sexual Alchemy, sexual energy (qi) is viewed as a vital life force. Taoists believe that cultivating, conserving, and harmonizing sexual energy can enhance longevity, health, and spiritual enlightenment. In Shinto, the indigenous spirituality of Japan, there is no emphasis on sexual sin or guilt; instead, sexuality is seen as part of life and nature. It is considered a natural expression of vitality and the life force within humans and nature.

It is interesting to see how different the treatment of our sexuality has been in the Western World to those of our Eastern cousins, where it is believed that if our sexuality centre is out of balance, our entire wellbeing will suffer. Instead, in our more 'civilised' cultures, our sexual selves are treated with far less attention and care. People have had to convert their sexuality into something that would fit into conventional boxes. The consequences have been dire.

"The individual has to survive her sexuality; so sexuality has to be convertible. Conversion works, in Freud's account, by estranging us from our desire, from our real enjoyment, but with other pleasures. Conversion for Freud is the best picture of the worst kind of adaptation: the sacrificing of sexual pleasure in the service of psychic survival." ~ Adam Phillips[2]

I find it so incredibly sad that sexuality has been something that we have felt we must 'survive' rather than something that was always meant to help us thrive. And yet, I, too, find it to have been my experience to date. When I was growing up, sexuality was a taboo topic, and any girl confident with hers was labelled a slut. Our sexual sides were never talked about, and therefore, there was no guidance on what sexuality was and how to connect with it in healthy, safe ways. At school, we got the mandatory and very mundane lessons about menstruation, sex and sin. The key takeaway from these talks was that masturbation was evil, sex was only ever for procreation (not pleasure) and was to be reserved for marriage, and any other matters should be discussed with your doctor. In those days, doctors were largely men, and the surgery did not feel like a safe space at all to discuss reproductive health.

Growing up, I had no frameworks, scientific studies or spiritual guides to lean on to help me understand my body or behaviours or how this essence fitted within my external existence. There was also no internet (what, no Google!) to interrogate. I learnt through what I saw in mainstream media and popular culture and from the more 'advanced' girls, which all merely resulted in despair about my own deficiencies. I also learnt many lessons about what I "should" be from boyfriends, and without any objective perspectives, I realise now how often my innate sexuality became a source of shame. I suspect this is the case for so many people, and it created so much harm.

I am no expert in biology, anthropology, mental health or modernity. Nor am I some fabulous feminist who inspires with vision and verve. However, over my many years, I have realised that with each that passes, I enlarge my expertise in what it means to be human. With additional years of my life,

I understand the longing for self-knowledge and have come to realise, as Carl Jung so poignantly puts it, that sexuality is an essential part of this pursuit.

"Sexuality is only one of the life-instincts – only one of the psycho-physiological functions – though one that is without doubt very far-reaching and important." ~ Carl Jung[3]

The World Health Organisation (WHO) states that sexuality is a central aspect of being human[4]. So, without seeking to understand it, any insight into ourselves will be incomplete; without tapping into this innate intelligence, we will remain partially ignorant. While our wobbly bits may wither away, the desire to know ourselves fully does not; therefore, the need to delve into our sexual selves does not deteriorate either. It merely changes with the context.

"And that little fire
Is still alive in me
It will never go away."
~ Madonna (This Used to be My Playground).

There is another profound reason for researching your sexuality at any age, and that is for love.

"True love requires deep understanding. In fact, love is another name for understanding. If you do not understand, you cannot love properly. Without understanding, your love will only cause the other person to suffer."
~ Thich Nhat Hanh

Whether we are seeking to love ourselves more or give greater love to others, we must first appreciate our totality, even the bits that challenge us. We must find a way to understand, acknowledge, and appreciate our sexuality so that we can offer ourselves and others a more conscious connection and create a space for compassion in this crazy world.

As the title suggests, the purpose of this book is to explore the notion of sexuality from every angle so that we can find our own truth and then live it fully.

"The privilege of a lifetime is to become who you truly are."
~ Carl Jung.

It has taken me all my life (so far) to come to an understanding of what sexuality is and the role it plays in my life. I have had decades of research, some theoretical and many practical, and I made many errors and wrong turns along the way. It is my privilege now to document the frameworks, facts and reflections that have helped me make sense of it all. These are the lessons that have fostered a sense of belonging within and admiration for my sexuality. I only hope they may aid you in coming to adore your authenticity and bring compassion to your complexity.

To achieve this, in these pages, we will investigate:

- Our Sexual Self – our unique mix of physical form, gender, attraction, desire and pleasure.

- Sexual fluidity – how our sexual selves shift and change over time.
- How our sexuality fosters connections with others.
- Sexuality as a key link to spirituality.
- How maturity affects our sexuality.
- The consequences of melding sexuality and morality.
- The modern authorities of our sexuality and the impact they are having on this sacred power.

This book explores sexuality through the holistic dimensions of body, mind, emotion and spirit. It delves deeper than just the tangible aspects of butts and boobs to understand it's inherent power. Because as you will see, sexuality may be manifest in the physical, but it is driven by the spiritual. To tap into its power, we need to move from the mundane aspects that modernity focuses upon to the magical, sacred and spiritual that fuel its expression in the world.

As you will notice, this book contains many quotes and lyrics from Madonna. This is intentional, as Madonna was my very first role model for what it meant to be confident in your own skin. She stands as a powerful example of understanding, accepting, and growing into one's authentic sexuality. Madonna has continually pushed boundaries, celebrating sexual freedom and self-expression while challenging societal norms. For those like myself who may experience anxiety around ageing, Madonna's unapologetic embrace of her evolving identity serves as a beautiful reminder that sexuality is not bound by age but is something that can be lived and expressed at every stage of life. Therefore, this book also pays tribute to Madonna as someone who has invested their spirit in understanding sexuality.

Chapter 1 – What Is Sexuality?

It is recognised that sexuality is a central aspect of being human[5]. However, sexuality is more important than being just one part of our precious whole; it is the reason for our very existence. All life on this planet is formed from a sexual union, a coming together of energies to bring about creation. For such an encompassing concept, though, we invest very little time investigating it and even less having intelligent conversations about it.

Perhaps it is because the word includes 'sex' that we consider it untouchable or taboo. However, continuing to ignore it, reject or downplay how much it influences our lives prevents us from building strong and positive relationships with ourselves and others. It creates the risk of us being swept away with what is socially acceptable rather than being grounded in our truth.

So, what is sexuality? Some authors propose the subject is too complex for one consistent definition and advocate that ambiguity is acceptable. Yes, sexuality is an intricate web of complicated components. I acknowledge it is multidimensional, with each dimension influenced by a multitude of personal circumstances and cultural factors. Yes, I agree sexuality is an inherently individual experience that is difficult to express fully in words. However, as stated by Graeber and Wengrow:

"One must simplify the world to discover something new about it."[6]

Without a common language and simple, shared concepts, the opportunity to have full and frank conversations with yourself, your partners and your children is lost. Understanding is compromised, and so, as we have heard from Thich Nhat Han, is the opportunity for love.

The Definition of Sexuality?

Sexuality is not just important, but it's a vital aspect of our lives. It permeates numerous contexts and can hold a myriad of meanings. However, while ambiguity allows for individual interpretation, a lack of clarity can hinder communication and connection, leading to cynicism, conflict and separation. The ultimate goal, then, is to build a shared foundation of what sexuality is. This can then be a framework that each individual can use to explore their own truths and build a deeper understanding of themselves.

Like any robust model, a framework of sexuality must begin with definitions. From all of my reading and personal experience, I have developed the following definition of sexuality:

Sexuality is the relationship between our physical bodies and the thoughts, feelings and behaviours that we use to form intimate connections.

What is imperative to understand in this definition is that the connections referred to are not just with other people. They include the relationship we form with:

- Ourselves.
- The creatures we come across.
- The spaces and energies we exist within.

Sexuality, then, is not just how we attract and interact with other people. It is a gift we can use to develop deep and meaningful mateship with ourselves. It is also the energy we use to interact with other people, creatures and places.

While this definition of sexuality makes sense to me, I don't expect it to resonate with everyone. In fact, if you disagree with my definition, that's a fantastic result; it means you now have a starting point to develop your view of what sexuality means for you.

The Two Elements of Sexuality

As the previous definition suggests, there are two main aspects to our sexuality: what we have and how we share this with others. These two elements are known as:

1. The Sexual Self.
2. Sexual Connection.

These two dimensions of sexuality are described beautifully by Alexandra Solomon in her book *Taking Sexy Back*[7]. However, instead of Solomon's term Sexual Agency, I have chosen to use the term Sexual Self as it is a term that is much more understandable and somewhat more personal.

Very simply, the Sexual Self is the set of things that are true to us, representing who we really are. Sexual Connection is how our Sexual Self is expressed in intimate relationships with all other forms of life.

The following diagram, which has been cheekily christened the Sexuality Circle, shows the key elements of sexuality.

Figure 1 - The Sexuality Circle

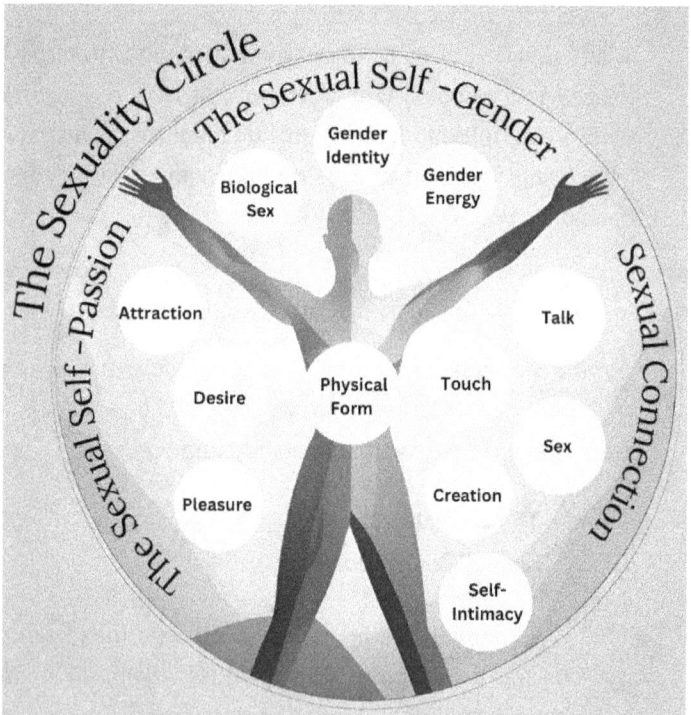

The Physical Form

At the core of the Sexuality Circle lies the Physical Form. It is through our bodies that we experience and express sexuality, making the Physical Form an essential foundation for both the Sexual Self and Sexual Connection. Our bodies are more than just biological vessels; they are the meeting point where physical sensations, emotional experiences, and intimate interactions converge. The Physical Form allows us to feel attraction, experience desire, and explore pleasure.

Recognising the body's importance in sexuality is crucial. We connect with ourselves and others through our senses—touch, sight, sound, taste, and smell. Our skin, nerve endings, and hormones interact with the world around us, translating external stimuli into internal experiences. These experiences shape our understanding of intimacy, vulnerability, and self-awareness.

However, the Physical Form is not merely a passive participant in sexuality. It also represents the potential for empowerment and self-expression. The body can become a canvas on which we paint our desires and advertise our boundaries. Learning to understand and respect our physical form—its needs, limitations, and pleasures—creates the foundation for a deep sense of intimacy with ourselves and meaningful sexual connections with others.

At the intersection of sexuality and physicality, the body serves as both the catalyst for and the recipient of intimate experiences. As we explore the dynamics of the Sexual Self and Sexual Connection, it is vital to honour the body not as an afterthought but as the central piece in our understanding of what it means to be a sexual being. Our bodies ground us, providing the physical space to express our true selves and allowing us to share that authenticity with others. The more conscious and compassionate we are towards our own physical form, the more we can bring these qualities to our relationships.

The Sexual Self

The Sexual Self, as the name suggests, is all about you. It includes all the elements that make up your unique, quirky, magical mosaic. They include:

Gender

Biological sex - what you were born with. That is the set of chromosomes and genitalia you came into the world with. Some people know biological sex as gender or just sex (e.g. male or female).

Gender identity - can be the same or different as your biological sex. It is your sense of self as a man or woman, both or neither. Some common categories include cisgender (has a gender identity the same as your biological sex), transgender (identifies as a gender different to your biological sex) and gender non-binary (does not identify as either male or female).

Gender energy - an inner, psychological quality or character essence[8]. Gender energy describes the psychological traits, characteristics, personal goals and preferences typically associated with masculinity or femininity. While there is a small proportion of balanced people, and there is a fluctuation between both depending upon the context, most people tend towards masculine or feminine energy in their everyday lives.

Passion

Attraction - the gender identities, energies, appearances and personality traits you feel drawn to connect with. In terms of gender identities, attractions can be for the opposite sex (what we know as heterosexual or 'straight'), the same-sex (homosexual or gay), or pansexual (which is flexible in terms of identity attraction).

Desire - how much you want intimate connection. It is also known as libido. The possibilities here range from no desire (asexual) to high sexual desire. It is important to note that just like most other elements of sexuality, this one changes over time.

Pleasure - what makes YOU feel good. This element is often missed or belittled in discussions of sexuality, but it is of vital importance. Once you understand your attitudes towards pleasure and what feels good to you, then you can have the ability to create intimate connections that are honest and mutually satisfying.

Self-intimacy - some would call this solo sex or masturbation. I think both terms are extremely limiting and have negative connotations. I prefer the term self-intimacy because that is exactly what it is - getting close to, understanding and being comfortable with your body.

Through self-intimacy, you also come to understand the areas of your body that bring you pleasure, and this knowledge is powerful. By demeaning self-intimacy, we also deny ourselves the ability to love our sexual nature.

Sexual Connection

At some point, the elements of our sexuality will have the opportunity to connect with those of another person. We then have the chance to talk, touch, create with and have close body contact. The coming together of the two sexualities may lead to sex, or it may not. There can be a beautiful exchange of energies even without exposure of the genitals.

Nevertheless, sex also therefore requires a definition. Here is mine:

Sex is the act of stimulating the sexual organs for pleasure and/or procreation.

This definition recognises that because of the diverse nature of the participants, there is a wide variety of what sex looks like. We need to acknowledge it as something more than just penis-in-vagina penetration, while also respecting the notion of sex as involving the ultimate vulnerability. By widening the definition of sex, it also allows us to begin conversations with our children about sexual health, even before they engage in intercourse.

I have shown talk and touch as key elements of sexual connection because I think it is important to acknowledge these as pleasurable and meaningful sources of intimate exchange. Unfortunately, these are often overshadowed by the obsessive pursuit of sex, which I will discuss in more detail later. Creation has been noted as a form of sexual connection, and this can be as simple as starting a herb garden together, renovating a kitchen, building a business, writing a book, or caring for pets. I have deemed creation a form of sexual connection because it is the coming together of masculine and feminine energies to bring forth something unique and valuable. Procreation, bringing forth the life of a child, is one form of creation, but between people, there are many others that also need to be recognised as sacred sexual activities.

Previously, I have also mentioned the ability to make intimate connections with spaces and places, energies and all forms of existence. I think that this is an important concept of sexuality that is often overlooked. In interacting with other people, we exchange energy, open ourselves to each other, and share our spirits. I believe we also have this ability to intertwine with every presence around us. We can move with the water, with the wind, on the earth, within space and in the light of the sun, moon and stars. We can allow these elements to touch us on every level and touch them in return. Our sexuality then also can create connections with both our physical and ethereal environment.

Sexual Fluidity

Apart from our biological sex, all of the elements of the Sexual Self can fluctuate over time. Every piece of research proves it - our gender energy, who we are attracted to, our level of desire and things that provide pleasure are all changeable over the course of our lives.

In our thirst for certainty, we would like to cling to one way of being, a single definition of our sexuality across our lifetime. But let's get real - this is not the way it works. We are complex, changeable and sometimes contradictory. We are sexually fluid creatures; our sexuality ebbs and flows. Sexual fluidity is the term used to describe this changeable characteristic, and it is becoming an increasing part of the common lexicon.

I am not sure 'sexual fluidity' is the best term to describe the phenomenon of changeability, as it seems to denote a sense of purposeless drifting. I believe our bodies, minds, and spirits are wiser than that; they do not simply allow us to wander. I believe we all have an innate sense of wisdom, one that knows what we need at any one time to accelerate our growth. All the plants on this earth know what they need to thrive, so why shouldn't our human bodies, minds and spirits have at least this level of intelligence? However, regardless of terminology, the fact that we are finally acknowledging that our sexuality is not a stable, stagnant set of traits is a breakthrough.

Our Modern Distorted View of Sexuality

While the term Sexuality Circle may be a little crass, the use of circles in the model is meaningful. It enables a clear depiction of what happens when one or more elements of sexuality become distorted and how the entire system can become unbalanced. I see this happening when the focus of our sexuality is placed on the one single act of sex.

Sex is an incredibly special part of sexuality and holds so much potential for creating profound and pleasurable connections. The problem we have today, which will be discussed in greater detail later, is that not only do we equate sexual connection with sex, but we also then seek to have sex mimic porn, which we may believe portrays successful sex.

So, by association, we come to the following conclusions:

Sexuality = sexual connection

Sexual connection = sex

Sex = porn

Therefore

Sexuality = porn.

These narrow and misguided interpretations of sexuality and sex corrupt the sacred nature of this power. Instead of treasuring our truth, we are more likely to be trying to live up to what media tells us is 'sexy'. The new wave of women baring all and singing about their sexual prowess may be a consequence of this distorted view. They do little to actually empower women and girls, for their force is creating competition and conflict rather than connection. The mangled view of our sexuality, where it becomes equated with sex and porn, is shown in the following diagram.

Figure 2 - Our Modern Distorted View of Sexuality

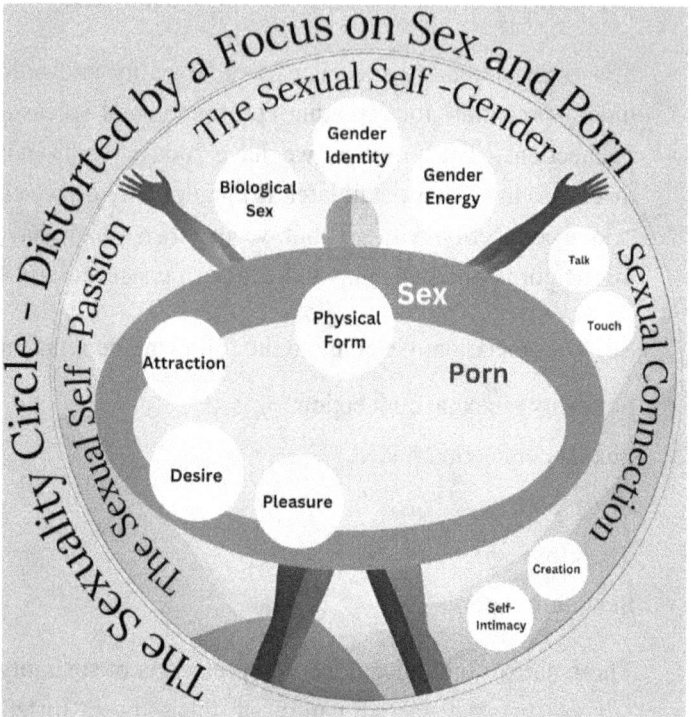

This perspective pervades so many aspects of our lives. It seeps through the dances and relationship dramas on social media, the lyrics we hear on the radio, and the love scenes in films. It is also found in the characters our children encounter in online games, where they are over-sexualised and seek out others for self-validation.

The consequence of this unbalanced view is that the pursuit of Sexual Connection becomes prioritised. It overtakes the significance of our Sexual Self, and our preferences get pushed out. We lose ourselves in the longing to make intimate connections with another and validate our self-worth. We compromise our truth for the sake of convenient connections. Using porn as a measure of what successful sex looks like also pussifies our power and compromises what such connections could be.

Sexuality and Spirituality

Our sexuality, however, does not operate in a contained circle. It is both shaped by and shapes a broader energy known as spirituality. As is shown in the following diagram, spirituality does not equal religion. People may subscribe to doctrines of a shared belief, but this is not the totality of what comprises their spirituality. I define spirituality as the:

Practice of connecting with and enacting the unique set of purpose, values, passions and gifts you bring into this world.

The addition of the Spirituality Circle shows us that our sexuality is influenced by the beliefs we inherit from our families, the morals imposed by our communities, and the role models we see on social media. All of these things can support us in knowing and living our unique sexual selves, but they can also subvert our spirits and have us trying to comply with conflicting standards. Owning your sexuality, then, is a process of identifying those things you have inherited from the outside circle that are actually important to you, and which ones you need to let go of and unlearn to enable your true self to shine.

Figure 3 - Sexuality and Spirituality

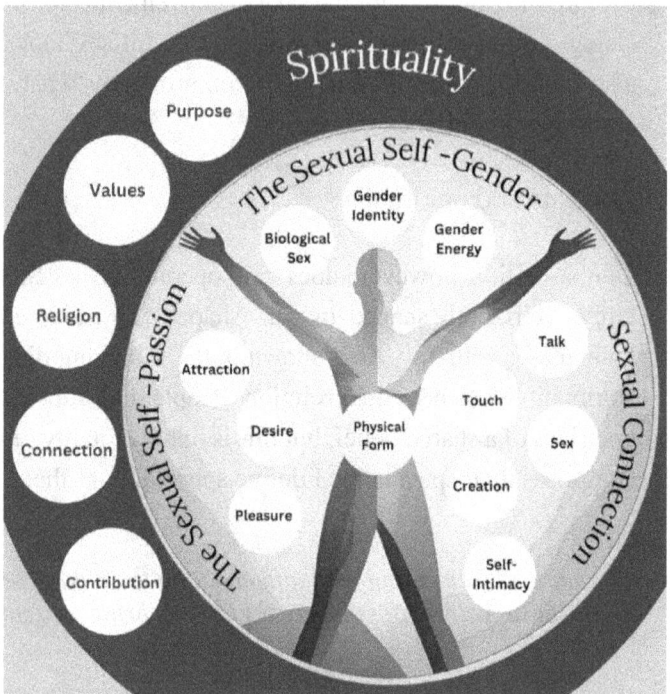

The Spirituality Circle also calls us to consider how our sexuality can be used to make a unique and positive contribution to this world by:

- **Being true to ourselves** - coming to know and connect with our authentic spirit, our internal sources of wisdom and power.
- **Being true to something bigger than ourselves** - being aware of and uniting with a greater strength, be it in a partnership, community, nature, a higher power or the universal divine.

Sexual Freedom

This chapter has provided a simple model that may help you better understand sexuality—the Sexuality Circle. The Sexuality Circle shows that each person has a unique combination of gender identity and energy, as well as specific things they find attractive, desire, and find pleasurable. Therefore, when we think about the notion of sexual freedom, it is realised when an individual can:

- Understand and appreciate their unique traits.
- Feel comfortable in expressing and sharing their special sexuality.
- Be aware that their sexuality may flow and fluctuate over time, and not judge themselves for any changes that ensue.

Now, let's explore the elements of the Sexuality Circle in more detail and explore what feels right for you at this time.

Core Concepts

Sexuality is fundamental to human existence yet we often avoid discussing it openly.

While sexuality is multifaceted and complex, having simple, shared concepts helps foster understanding of a person's own and others unique perspectives.

Sexuality is the relationship between our physical bodies and the thoughts, feelings, and behaviours that form intimate connections, both with ourselves and others.

Sexuality includes two elements: the Sexual Self (who we are) and Sexual Connection (how we share ourselves with others).

Our bodies are central to how we experience sexuality through senses like touch, sight, and sound, making the physical form a key component of sexual identity.

Sexuality is fluid and changes over time, with elements like gender identity, attraction, and desire evolving throughout life.

Modern society distorts sexuality by reducing it to sex and equating it with pornography, undermining the true power of the Sexual Self and Sexual Connection.

Sexuality is deeply connected to spirituality, which involves aligning with your purpose, values, and passions, adding depth to sexual experiences.

Chapter 2 – The Physical Form

"And I said to my body softly, 'I want to be your friend.' It took a long breath and replied, 'I have been waiting my whole life for this.'" ~ Nayyirah Waheed

When we talk about the physical form in the context of sexuality, we're not just referring to our anatomy. While our biological makeup—our organs, skin, bodily systems, boobs and butts—plays a crucial role in our sexual experiences, the physical form encompasses much more. Through our senses, we experience the world around us, and both desire and connection are embodied emotions; we feel these states within. We use our bodies to express attraction, pleasure, and even vulnerability. In this sense, the physical form is the gateway to our sexual selves. Our bodies act as:

- A sensor.
- A messenger.
- A connector.
- A form of self-expression.

The Body As A Sensor

In the realm of sexuality, the body's role as a sensor is especially significant. The sensory experiences we take in— whether it's the sound of a bird song, the smell of someone's skin, or the softness of a fabric or a lover's embrace—are central to how we engage with our sexual selves. These sensory inputs activate different areas of our brain, intertwining the physical with the emotional and psychological. For example, a simple caress can evoke feelings of trust, intimacy, and desire, while a familiar scent might reignite memories of a past connection or create a powerful new attraction. Our senses play a critical role in shaping the depth of our sexual and emotional experiences, transforming physical touch into meaningful and intimate moments.

Through this constant interplay of sensory information, the body not only receives signals but also interprets and responds to them, helping us connect to our sexual selves and others in profound ways.

The Body As A Messenger

Our bodies are powerful messengers, constantly giving us insight into what is going on for us physically, mentally and emotionally. When we are aligned with what feels right—whether it's a decision, a relationship, or an intimate experience—our bodies respond positively. We might feel sensations of warmth, openness, or ease. In contrast, when we are moving away from what feels authentic to us, our bodies send clear signals of discomfort. This can manifest as tension, anxiety, or a sense of dissociation or disconnect. By tuning in to these physical cues, we can better understand what brings us comfort or discomfort and use this information to make choices that honour our true selves. In this way, our bodies act as a compass, guiding us toward what feels right and away from what does not. Our bodies are more than just vessels; they are guides towards finding our authentic sexuality.

The Body As A Connector

Our bodies serve not only as messengers and sensors but also as powerful connectors. In the realm of sexuality, the body is the medium through which we form intimate, emotional, and physical bonds with others. It is through touch, presence, and physical closeness that we create connections that transcend words, enabling deeper levels of trust, affection, and understanding. The body becomes the bridge that allows us to share our vulnerabilities and desires with another person, fostering intimacy that goes beyond the surface.

Touch, in particular, is one of the most primal and meaningful ways we connect with others. Whether it's a gentle handhold, a hug, a stroke of the cheek, or a more intimate encounter, touch allows us to communicate feelings that words cannot always capture. A simple embrace can convey comfort, love, or support, while a more intimate touch can stir desire and passion. Our bodies enable this nonverbal communication, helping us build bonds that are rooted in both physical and emotional intimacy.

However, the body also connects us in ways that extend beyond individual relationships. It ties us to our surroundings and to the energies of the world around us. When we are present in our bodies, we can feel connected to the environment—whether it's the grounding sensation of bare feet on the earth, the warmth of sunlight on our skin, or the calming rhythm of our own breath. This connection to the physical world can create a sense of belonging, reminding us that we are part of something larger than ourselves.

Furthermore, the body allows us to connect to ourselves. Through self-touch, self-care, and mindful awareness of our physical form, we can deepen the relationship we have with our own being. This connection fosters self-love, self-acceptance, and a deeper understanding of our desires and boundaries. The more we are in tune with our bodies, the more connected we become to our true selves, enabling us to share that authenticity with others in our relationships.

The Body As A Form Of Self-Expression

Our bodies are not only physical vessels but also powerful tools for expressing who we are. Through the choices we make about how we present and adorn our physical form, we communicate aspects of our identity, values, and desires. In the realm of sexuality, this self-expression often takes on even greater significance, as it allows us to define and claim our own sexual identity in ways that are deeply personal.

One of the most intimate forms of self-expression is the choice surrounding pubic hair. While body hair has long been influenced by cultural and societal standards, how we choose to groom or embrace our body hair can be a deeply personal decision. For some, keeping or growing their pubic hair is a way of reclaiming natural beauty and rejecting external pressures to conform to hair removal trends. For others, grooming or removing pubic hair is tied to comfort, hygiene, or aesthetics. There's no "right" choice when it comes to pubic hair—what matters is that the decision feels true to the individual, allowing them to express their body in a way that aligns with their identity and sense of sexuality.

Similarly, piercings have long been used as a form of self-expression, allowing people to adorn their bodies and highlight particular features. Piercings, whether on the ears, nose, nipples, or elsewhere, can carry deep cultural, spiritual, or personal significance. For some, body piercings represent milestones, individuality, or rebellion against societal norms. In a sexual context, piercings can enhance one's relationship with their body, making one feel empowered, beautiful, or daring. Like choices around pubic hair, piercings give us a way to shape how we want to be seen by the world and how we connect with our own sense of sexuality.

Tattoos, too, are a powerful form of body-based self-expression. A tattoo is not just ink on skin—it's a visual statement of something meaningful to the wearer. Whether chosen for aesthetic reasons, symbolic meaning, or personal significance, tattoos tell a story. They can represent an important life event, a personal philosophy, or even a connection to one's sexuality. For some, getting a tattoo is an act of claiming ownership over their body, using it as a canvas to express their unique journey or identity. In terms of sexuality, tattoos can make someone feel more confident, attractive, or connected to their body in new ways.

What all of these choices—whether around pubic hair, piercings, or tattoos—have in common is the opportunity for self-expression. They give us agency over our bodies, allowing us to present ourselves in a way that aligns with our personal values, identity, and sense of self. In a world where many of us feel pressure to conform to external standards of beauty or sexuality, making intentional choices about our bodies becomes an act of reclaiming power. By expressing ourselves through these physical forms, we are able to communicate to the world—and to ourselves—who we truly are and how we want to be seen.

When Our Bodies Become A Battleground

The reality is that for many, the physical form is not a source of pleasure but of pain. There are those who do not see their body as a gift, but as something to be measured and judged. Instead of being a source of expression, connection, and joy, the body becomes a war zone—pitted against unrealistic standards, societal pressures, and our own feelings of shame. This internal conflict leads to an ongoing struggle with body image, self-worth, and identity, often with dangerous consequences.

One of the most insidious aspects of this war with the self is comparison. In a world flooded with idealised images and expectations—whether through social media, advertisements, or cultural norms—we are constantly bombarded with messages about what our bodies *should* look like. When we inevitably fall short of these impossible ideals, shame often takes root. We start to see our bodies not as sources of strength or pleasure but as objects of failure. They no longer become mediums for enlightenment but evidence of our inferiority.

This shame leads us to view our bodies as something to be fixed or corrected. We begin scrutinising every flaw, real or imagined, and internalising the belief that we are somehow inadequate or unworthy because of how we look. This cycle of comparison and shame can manifest in numerous harmful ways. Some may resort to extreme dieting, disordered eating, or over-exercising in an attempt to change their appearance. Others may engage in risky cosmetic procedures, chasing a version of beauty that they believe will make them more lovable, accepted, or valued.

Currently, over one-quarter of young men and over one-third of young women are critical of their appearance. Conditions such as body dysmorphia, anxiety, and depression can also develop as a result of this toxic relationship with the body and cases are rising rapidly. Body dysmorphia, for instance, occurs when an individual becomes obsessively preoccupied with perceived flaws in their appearance, often seeing themselves as ugly or deformed despite there being no evidence to support this view. Their perception of imperfection becomes a rigid reality. This distorted view of oneself can lead to a relentless pursuit of physical manipulation and improvement, leaving the individual constantly dissatisfied and disconnected from their true worth.

The danger of seeing the body as a battleground is that it diminishes our ability to connect with ourselves and others. When we are consumed by shame and comparison, it becomes difficult to appreciate the unique beauty of our own physical form. We may also find it challenging to fully engage in intimate relationships, as feelings of insecurity and inadequacy undermine our confidence and willingness to share ourselves with others. It is difficult to reach out to another when you are afraid of relaxing your source of protection. The body becomes a source of anxiety rather than pleasure, a barrier rather than a bridge to connection.

What's more, when we are at war with our bodies, we lose sight of the fact that they are not just objects to be moulded into societal ideals but living, breathing expressions of who we are. We forget that our bodies have their own wisdom, that they are capable of experiencing pleasure, carrying us through life, and forming connections with others. The more we battle against our physical form, the more disconnected we become from its power, its beauty, from others and the world around us.

Ultimately, to bring peace to our physical form, we must shift our perspective. We need to stop viewing our bodies as projects to be perfected or compared and instead see them as vital, dynamic parts of who we are. By embracing our bodies with compassion and respect, we can reclaim the space they hold in our lives, allowing them to be sources of strength, connection, and self-expression rather than shame and conflict.

"Step away from the mean girls and say bye-bye to feeling bad about your looks. Are you ready to stop colluding with a culture that makes so many of us feel physically inadequate? Say goodbye to your inner critic, and take this pledge to be kinder to yourself and others." ~ Oprah

---

Core Concepts

Our bodies are sensors, guiding us toward what feels right through physical cues like warmth, joy or ease.

Sensory experiences—touch, sound, and smell—play a key role in engaging with our sexual selves and shaping emotional and sexual connections.

Our bodies act as connectors, enabling intimacy and communication through touch, creating bonds that transcend words.

Our physical forms connect us not only to others but also to the environment, reminding us of the reality of interdependence.

Through mindfulness of our bodies and self-care, we can connect deeply with ourselves, fostering self-love and understanding of our desires and boundaries.

Our bodies can play a key role in self-expression, empowering us to present ourselves in ways that align with our personal values.

Comparison and societal pressures can lead to shame about our bodies, damaging our ability to connect with ourselves, others, and to make our greatest contribution to this world.

Chapter 3 – The Sexual Self: Overview

Adam Phillips, in his book *Missing Out*, suggests that:

"You can know a person, but the one thing you cannot, in any real sense know, is their sexuality; partly because they do not know about it themselves; and partly because it is not the kind of thing that can be known."

I do not share one iota of Mr Phillips's intellect, but I will be so bold as to disagree with part of this proposition. I concur that many people do not know about their sexuality, but I decline to believe that it is because sexuality is something that cannot be known. I believe that with self-awareness, we can begin to appreciate the specific and special traits that combine to form our Sexual Self. Perhaps it is easier to find some sympathy for this view if we think of our sexuality as our sexual personality.

The concept of personality is well understood and appreciated in modern psychology, and mountains of self-help books help people discover theirs. One can work through renowned frameworks such as the Myers-Briggs, Big Five and DISC profiles that help us define our preferred way of working in the world. Therefore, I would suggest that the problem does not lie in our inability to know our sexuality but in the lack of support available to assist people to understand it.

Specifically, this lack of support is evidenced by:

- An absence of models of sexuality by which one can delve into its dimensions.
- The misconception that our sexuality only relates to sex, with the focus of understanding placed solely on this specific and simplistic segment.
- A focus on consent for connection rather than comprehension and compassion for the complete human being.
- People's preference for pigeonholing themselves into black-and-white categories prevents them from appreciating their personalities' dazzling dichotomies and gorgeous grey areas.
- A lack of encouragement for safe experimentation. Sometimes, you can only find out who you are by first discovering who you are not. Learning about ourselves requires interaction with others, but many people appear reluctant to try new things and evaluate their experiences.

Our Sexual Self also shares a number of features with our more well-recognised and overarching personality:

- **It is greatly affected by environmental influences**. This may make it difficult to determine whether the sexual personality you identify is your authentic self or is the one that you think is seen to be preferable by parents or peers. As you work through the following elements, see if you can distinguish between what you are told is proper versus what truly feels right for you.

- **It is changeable**. Just like our overarching personality, some elements of sexuality will remain relatively stable over time while others may shift substantially. Know that this version of your Sexual Self may evolve over time, but self-awareness and acceptance are gifts that last a lifetime.

- **Every sexuality is unique**. While some traits will be common across individuals, the specific combination of characteristics and the intensity to which they are expressed will vary from one person to another. Just like no one has the same personality as you, there is not another person on this planet with an identical sexuality.

I do agree, though, that as Adam Phillips goes on to say:

"Parents might know their children very well but they may know very little about their children's desire, and of course, vice versa."

We keep parts of our personality hidden from others, and it is the same with our sexual selves. We do this for many reasons, including:

- Concern about the reactions from others.
- Uncertainty about how we feel or what we like.

- A preference to keep cherished parts of our personality for ourselves.

Nevertheless, I believe it is a noble pursuit for each person to understand their sexuality and celebrate it as a core part of their complete being. Working through the elements of Sexuality Circle and identifying what is true for us leads us to gain the gifts of self-awareness and self-acceptance. Knowing our Sexual Self also creates the opportunity for better decision-making, improved communication, and enhanced relationships. Knowing your Sexual Self is the first step to making changes in your life that can bring greater authenticity, freedom, and power.

Core Concepts

Sexuality can be understood through exploration and reflection.

There is a lack of support, models, and safe environments to help people explore and understand their sexual selves.

People often seek to categorise themselves into black-and-white definitions, missing the unique nuances of their sexual personalities.

Safe experimentation and self-reflection are key to discovering what feels right or wrong for us, but many are hesitant to explore new aspects of their sexuality.

Sexuality is shaped by environmental influences, making it important to distinguish between authentic desires and those shaped by societal expectations.

Like overall personality, sexuality can change over a lifetime, with some aspects remaining stable while others evolve with experience.

Also like our personalities, every person's sexuality is unique, with no identical combination of traits and expressions.

UNDERSTANDING SEXUALITY

Chapter 4– The Sexual Self: Gender

Gender is a deeply personal aspect of who we are. It shapes how we see ourselves, how we relate to others, and how we express ourselves in the world. In this chapter, we will explore the three key components of gender: biological sex, gender identity, and gender energy. Biological sex refers to the physical attributes we are born with, while gender identity reflects our internal understanding of ourselves as male, female, both, or neither. Finally, gender energy is a form of expression, a mix of masculine and feminine motivations and behaviours that influence how we move through life. Together, these elements create the complex and unique gender experience each of us embodies.

Biological Sex

On the surface, gender is a very simple concept. There are two sexes for our species, male and female. This binary notion is the concept known as sexual dimorphism - the recognition that there are only two genders. However, thanks to so many scientists who have been investigating sexuality in more detail, we now understand that it is far more complex. It appears to be so much more than just the combination of X and Y chromosomes. It actually involves an intricate interplay between five factors: chromosomal, gonadal, hormonal, morphological, and behavioural aspects.

Chromosomal Sex: The sex determination of an individual based on their sex chromosomes. In many species, including humans, sex is determined by the presence of specific sex chromosomes. In mammals, females typically have two X chromosomes (XX), while males have one X and one Y chromosome (XY). These chromosomal differences play a fundamental role in developing the gonadal and hormonal aspects of sexual differentiation.

Gonadal Sex: The development of reproductive glands (gonads), which can become either ovaries or testes. The presence or absence of specific genes on the sex chromosomes (e.g., SRY gene in mammals) directs the development of gonads into either testes (which produce sperm) or ovaries (which produce eggs). Gonadal development is a critical step in sexual differentiation and determines the production of gametes (sperm or eggs).

Hormonal Sex: Hormonal sex involves the production and influence of sex hormones, such as testosterone and estrogen, which are secreted by the gonads. These hormones have profound effects on the development of secondary sexual characteristics, including body hair, breast development, and voice changes in humans. Hormones also play a role in regulating sexual behaviour and reproductive processes.

Morphological Sex: Refers to an organism's physical form and structure, including its external and internal sexual anatomy. It encompasses the presence of structures such as genitalia, mammary glands, and other secondary sexual characteristics. Morphological sex is often closely linked to gonadal and hormonal sex. It is responsible for the visual differences between males and females.

Behavioural Sex (Gender Identity). Relates to an individual's internal sense of their own gender and their behaviour in accordance with that gender identity. It encompasses how individuals perceive themselves and may identify as male, female, or non-binary, regardless of their chromosomal, gonadal, or morphological sex.

To simplify these concepts, I have grouped the first four elements of chromosomal, gonadal, hormonal and morphological elements under the term 'biological sex'. This category represents those things that can be observed and tested and that could be used to assign a gender. However, it is widely recognised that there is no such thing as specific male or female hormones. As we will see in the next chapter, all humans share the same set, just in differing amounts. Moreover, the sexual differentiation pathways are intimately linked, with the development of gender being described as an:

"Interconnected chaos of androgynous genes" and that "subtle tweaks in the expression of any of the interwoven cogs will produce novel variations."[9]

All of the elements of biological sex can influence each other but also conflict with one another, creating a whole spectrum of sexual makeup and expression. Dr Joan Roughgarden describes this as "evolution's rainbow."[10]

Even tiny changes in a myriad of any of the huge number of genes and hormones involved in sexual differentiation can radically alter a person's sexual trajectory. Thus, instead of the simple black-and-white view of gender, there is a great variety in what we know as our biological sex.

"Sex is not all black or white, and labelling grey areas as anomalies, or worse, pathologies – means we fail to appreciate the natural function of diversity."[11]

The outcome of this insight, as proposed by Professor David Crews, is that there are many types of 'intersex' between the masculine and feminine extremes and that we need to be rid of dualistic and archaic classifications of gender.

"We need to get away from the binary nature of sex assignment. There's a continuum, with males at one end and females at the other, and variability is continuous between those two types."[12]

The latest research would suggest that being at the complete end of any gender spectrum is rare and that many of us may be not fully, but mainly either male or female. Non-binary may be far more natural for humans than currently considered normal.

When we realise that gender is not a simple binary solution, biological sex becomes far less important to individual sexuality than what people feel is true to them. No longer is our understanding of gender cramped by cultural norms. And finally, we have a reason to ditch cultural biases that only result in differentiation and division. Science has given us permission to embrace the complexity and individuality of sexuality and the colour that it can bring to the world. We can take differences as a given and move on to the more important work of understanding our shared humanity.

Gender Identity

Nevertheless, as humans, we still find comfort in putting things in neat little boxes. We have also done this with gender identity. The options you hear being bandied about these days for gender identity include the following:

- Cisgender - has a gender identity the same as your biological sex.
- Transgender - identifies as a gender different to biological sex.
- Gender non-binary - does not identify as either male or female.

I am of two minds, though, when it comes to the existence of gender identity. I do believe having a shared language around sexuality is helpful. It does assist in classifying and comprehending ourselves and communicating who we are to other people. Hopefully, though, there will be a shift away from a focus on sexual identity over time. Because I worry about the downside of creating categories for gender identity, and that is the potential for them to fuel further social division. Sure, there may be some benefits from a social evolution and planning perspective to indicate categories on census surveys, and identification during medical treatment would be helpful for those called to care for us. Nevertheless, the longer we try to push people into clear containers, the more we continue to disrespect the intense individuality that is sexuality. Once we understand and appreciate the sexual spectrum, we can move beyond a focus on our differences and create conscious connections.

Gender Energy

It is interesting to see how the components of gender graduate from the tangible physical aspects to more inherent identities and finally to the subtle realm of energy. Our gender is comprised not only of what we have and who we believe we are but also of how we show up and contribute to the world; this is gender energy.

Gender energy: an inner, psychological quality or character essence[13].

Just like biological sex, you can think of gender energy existing along a continuum, with the masculine and feminine energies representing the extreme ends. Here's how the gender energies differ[14]:

Figure 4 - Gender Energies

	Feminine	Masculine[v]
Searching For	Deep love	Freedom
Find It in	Relationships	Challenges
Moved by	Connection	A mission or direction
Life feels like	A flow of emotion	A problem to be solved or art to be mastered
Thrives in	Giving and receiving love	Competition
Wants to	Flow with the energies of life	Transcend life and be free
Is lessened by	Hoping or searching for love	Struggling for freedom
Grows through	Learning to live as love	Learning to live as freedom

There are three important things to note about gender energy:

1. Gender energy has nothing to do with whether you identify as a woman or a man. Let's work through some examples. First, women in politics. Female politicians may have the biological sex and gender identity of a woman; however, their behaviour is incredibly masculine. They play power games to get free of others' influence. They are mission-driven and enjoy the competition of the question time arena. In contrast, let's look at some male nurses. They may have the bits of a boy, yet they spend their days building relationships, caring for and nurturing others and bringing love to their patients.

2. Gender energy is changeable. While a person may operate predominantly from one energy, we can move between them in a moment. A woman's masculine, competitive energy displayed on the sports field can be followed by profound care and love for her baby. A man's masculine energy directing troops on the battlefield can be followed by a heartfelt conversation with his teenager. It is this flow of energy that makes us human and not robots. We all have the capacity to act from a different energy. The question is whether we have the awareness and desire to know what energy is best in any specific situation.

3. Both energies are essential. The masculine energy is required to plan, push forward and make progress. The feminine energy is needed to nurture, rejuvenate and repair. The two need to exist in balance within each person and within a relationship. In recent human history, masculine energy has dominated, resulting in the relentless pursuit of progress and destruction of the planet. This imbalance has also relegated caring professions to be viewed as less valuable and substantially underpaid. It is argued that we need a swing towards the feminine to reconnect with our earth and create relationships with ourselves and others that will heal the planet.

Gender- From the Superficial to the Subtle

From these discussions, one thing has become incredibly clear. Gender is a very complex construct. It is an intricate interplay between:

- Our biological sex – the bits we were born with and the interplay between our hormones and genes.
- Our gender identity – how we categorise ourselves (and others categorise us) on the sexual spectrum.
- Our gender energy – the essence or character we use to express ourselves in the world and make connections.

For me, this understanding helps me realise that sexuality is so much more than just what you see on the surface. While we may consider gender as a function of what we see and what we say about ourselves, gender goes deep into the subtle layers of how we work in the world. Understanding our gender then means becoming intimate with every level of our existence.

Core Concepts

Gender is a multifaceted concept, shaping how we see ourselves, relate to others, and express ourselves. It includes the elements of biological sex, gender identity, and gender energy.

Biological sex encompasses chromosomal, gonadal, hormonal, and morphological factors, but these elements create a spectrum rather than a simple male/female binary.

Sexual dimorphism (the concept of two sexes) is oversimplified; biology shows that gender is more complex and variable than previously understood.

Gender identity reflects how we understand ourselves as male, female, both, or neither, and may not align with biological sex.

Gender energy is a psychological essence of masculinity or femininity, separate from biological sex or gender identity, representing how we show up in the world.

Gender energy fluctuates and changes depending on context, with both masculine and feminine energies being important for balance in life.

Societal labels for gender identity help us communicate who we are, but over-reliance on categories can create division and limit our understanding of the gender spectrum.

Chapter 5 – The Sexual Self: Passion

"Sexuality is the song of the body; it is what keeps us vibrant and alive, an expression of who we truly are at our core." — *Osho*

The next part of our Sexual Self is all about what brings us pleasure, whether this be what we admire in others in others, events that excite us or the desires that create a delectable dopamine hit. And just as the combination of biological sex, gender identity and gender energy are ultimately unique for every person, we all have passions that are particular to our individual sexual persona.

Attraction

Attraction means the gender identities, energies, physical forms and personality traits you feel drawn to connect with. There are some broad categories applied here as well. If you are attracted to the opposite sex, this is what we know as being heterosexual or straight. If you are drawn to the same sex, then you are said to be homosexual or gay. If you enjoy both men and women, then you are known as bi-sexual. However, suppose you do not discriminate between any gender or gender identity. In that case, you fit in the category of being pansexual. Asexuality is when you are not attracted on an intimate level to anyone at all.

But what are the factors that drive who and what we find appealing? Attraction is influenced by a combination of our unique biological sex, psychological traits, and cultural norms. Some of the key factors that contribute to sexual attraction include:

Physical Appearance

Physical features play a significant role in sexual attraction. These features can include gender, body shape, facial symmetry, skin tone, hair colour, and other physical characteristics. Evolutionary theories suggest that certain physical traits may be attractive because they signal health, fertility, and genetic fitness. For example, in a study by David Buss from the University of Michigan[15], it was found men preferred women who were young and beautiful. I guess there are no surprises here, particularly because these traits are associated with successful and sustained reproduction, and guys are historically hard-wired to strive to conquer the gene pool.

The definition of beauty, though, is a much malleable thing and is very much informed by our cultural norms. In Western Cultures, we have seen the pendulum swing from worshipping a full female figure in the Victorian Era to the stick-thin, pre-pubescent parade of models such as Twiggy in the 70s and Kate Moss in the 90s. Now the tide has turned again to the Kardashian standard of big butts and boobs. Despite what others tell us is beautiful, though, we will always have traits that we find tempting.

Personality Traits

Personality traits can greatly influence sexual attraction. The same study mentioned previously also found that both men and women preferred kindness and intelligence. Additionally, qualities such as confidence and humour create charisma. The traits that we find irresistible provide an insight into what we value and would like to have more of in our lives.

Scent and Pheromones

Human scent and pheromones can subconsciously influence attraction. Does this mean you should race out and buy big on the pheromone-based perfumes plastered all over TikTok? The short answer is no. These colognes are marketed with the claim that they can enhance a person's attractiveness to potential partners. However, scientific studies on the efficacy of commercial pheromone products have yielded mixed results. The reason is that attraction is a multifaceted phenomenon. Every other aspect discussed in this section will play a role in whether someone finds you attractive. The perfume may get their attention, but you will need more substance than scent to get your target to become fascinated with you.

Immunity Profiles

Interestingly, research suggests that people may be attracted to individuals with immune system profiles that complement their own, possibly detected through scent. It has been found that women are attracted to men with a Major Histocompatibility Complex (MHC) different from hers. This attraction is good for the species, as mating between people with different immunities means that the children benefit from a broader, more robust immune system. However, recently, it has been discovered that birth control pills interrupt this ability to detect the MHC of others. It short-circuits an important test of biological compatibility, and as a result, women begin to favour men with an immune system profile similar to their own.

As an aside, this outcome of contraception raises two pertinent questions for our relationships:

- **What happens when the woman goes off the pill?** For example, to have children. Do their smell receptors realign, also altering what they find attractive? Could this recalibration explain some people's experience of waking up one day and wondering what they saw in their partner in the first place?
- **Is there a relationship between oral contraceptive use and the increase in childhood allergies?** There certainly seems to be a correlation between the use of the pill and the proportion of children who are now experiencing allergies. Some preliminary studies have shown children whose mothers took the pill have a much higher rate of hay fever. It could be another example of humans messing with nature and creating many unintended consequences.

Chemistry and Hormones

Hormonal fluctuations can also impact attraction. For example, during ovulation, some women may be more attracted to masculine facial features, seemingly preparing the female for the opportunity to reproduce. Ultimately, we are pleasure-seeking creatures. Our brains are wired to move us towards the things that make us feel good and away from those that may harm or hinder our happiness. So, suppose you have had a past pleasurable experience with someone of a certain appearance or personality. In that case, neurotransmitters such as dopamine and serotonin will likely be released upon meeting someone similar. The memory creates a placeholder that will trigger our happy hormones and these push us towards repeating the previous pleasure.

Social Status and Resources

A study from the University of Michigan found that women listed wealth and status as their top criteria for choosing a partner. This preference is explained by evolutionary biology. Women make a great investment in the reproductive process. Their bodies are committed for several years, undertaking gestation, nurturing and feeding the child. It just makes sense that they would want to have a partner with sufficient resources to care for their family for the foreseeable future.

"Surely no-one has ever seriously doubted that men desire young beautiful women and that women desire wealthy, high-status men?"[16]

What is also fascinating is how, despite being attracted to a range of social levels, humans have a habit of sticking with people from the same social and economic background, a phenomenon known as Social Homogamy. People may experiment with moving up the social strata but tend to fall back to a familiar and comfortable level. This comfort comes from being around people with perceived common perspectives and goals. It may also be driven by either formal or unspoken social and cultural norms that set expectations around who should be together.

There are always some, though, who's main motivation is not financial support for their family but their self-esteem, and so they may use the other person's wealth to secure their own sense of self-worth.

Unique is Attractive

Many researchers in sexuality and evolutionary biology draw one conclusion about attraction: it is a bonus to be different. Here's what Charles Darwin had to say:

"If all our women were to become as beautiful as the Venus de Medici we should for a time be charmed, but we should soon wish for a variety; and as soon as we had obtained variety, we should wish to see certain characters in our women a little exaggerated beyond the then existing common standard."

Am I the only one thinking that Darwin predicted the dawn of cosmetic surgery and the extreme features (boobs, butts, lips and eyes) that we see comprising current beauty standards? It appears Darwin was both an evolutionary expert and a perceptive prophet.

In his book, *The Red Queen*, Matt Ridley goes further to suggest that it is not only our appearance but also our brains that evolve to entice.

"For no reason except that wit, virtuosity, inventiveness and individuality turn other people on. It is a somewhat less uplifting perspective on the purpose of humanity than the religious one, but it is also rather liberating. Be different."[17]

So, while social media may be flooded with images of an ideal mate, the message here is that there is a significant advantage to being unique. There will always be the fear of standing out in a crowd, and therefore, it is recognised that being authentic takes maturity and courage. However, it is also the foundation for rewarding relationships.

Desire

The definition of desire is:

"Having a strong feeling of wanting to have something or wishing for something to happen".

In this way, desire is the next step from attraction. Whereas attraction is seeing something of beauty and admiring and appreciating it for what it is, desire seeks to interact with this object in some way. Desire is the yearning to have something or do something. You may see a beautiful flower in the garden and find its presence pleasing. This is attraction – you are drawn to its appearance. However, if you are compelled to pick it, place it in a vase and possess it, then this is desire.

We may easily be confused between the desire for connection in this broader sense with the desire for sex, which is also called libido. But realistically, we can crave anything that pleases us, whether physical or psychological. We can yearn to talk to someone or for the touch of water. And just as with every other element of our Sexual Self, the levels and directions of our desires are unique to us. They are also dependent upon a number of both physical and psychological factors.

The Hormonal Influence

Hormones play a large role in our levels of desire at the physical level. The following chemicals play a crucial role in general mood and motivation, as well as, more specifically, in the search for sexual activity:

Testosterone: It is produced in the testes in men and in smaller amounts in the ovaries in women. It has been shown to affect the levels of neurotransmitters in the brain, including serotonin and dopamine, which play key roles in regulating mood.

Estrogen: Estrogen is produced primarily in the ovaries and helps maintain the health of the female reproductive organs, but it is also found in lower concentrations in men. Like testosterone, it plays a pivotal role in brain function and mood regulation.

Progesterone: Progesterone is produced mainly in the ovaries and is involved in regulating the menstrual cycle and supporting pregnancy; however, it is also found in males. Aside from its specific sexual health function, it also affects the central nervous system and can influence mood and stress responses.

Prolactin: Prolactin is a hormone produced by the pituitary gland. While it is best known for its role in assisting lactation in females, it also assists in adaptation to stress, regulating metabolism and sexual function.

Oxytocin: Oxytocin is released during positive physical interactions and enhances feelings of trust and empathy, promoting bonding between individuals.

Dopamine: Dopamine is a neurotransmitter that assists with anticipating and reinforcing rewards, motivating us to take pleasurable actions. Interestingly, it is also released in novel or uncertain situations, playing a role in exploration and learning.

Cortisol: Cortisol is a hormone the adrenal glands produce in response to stress. Chronic stress affects all aspects of our lives, negatively impacting our physical health and mental wellbeing and, as such, our desire and ability to enjoy intimate connections.

Thyroid Hormones: Thyroid hormones, including thyroxine (T4) and triiodothyronine (T3), are important for overall metabolic function and also regulate other key neurotransmitters. When they are too low, they can result in lethargy, and if they are too high, they can create anxiety.

The human body is a complex mix of these chemicals, and each and every person's makeup of them will be different. Moreover, as we age, our hormonal systems also shift and change, meaning that we will also experience our desire moving through different levels. Medicines can also impact the functioning of hormones, and so can have both advantages and disadvantages when it comes to feeling frisky!

The Psychological and Spiritual Factors

While the physical interaction of hormones in our bodies directly influences the degree of our desire, our psychological and even spiritual states also play a significant role in our sexual vitality. Healthy sexuality, then, is a function of holistic wellbeing.

When you look at heat maps of the body under various emotions, it is easy to see that the body lights up only when a person is experiencing happiness and love. Only in these two states is there a connection and flow between the body's energy centres. It is in this integrated state that Daniel Siegel would suggest true healing and health is possible[18].

If a person is sad or depressed, the genital regions are literally frozen, which gives a whole new perspective to the accusation of being 'frigid'. When we are angry, afraid, anxious, proud or ashamed, there is no activity in the sexual centres at all. In contrast, when we are in states of love and happiness, we are more open to sharing this with others physically and emotionally.

Happiness and love are found in the places where we are truly ourselves. They exist wherever we are seeking to grow and live to our fullest potential. They are found when:

- We feel safe.
- We are doing the things we love and are exploring our passions. That is, we are connected to our spirit.
- We feel connected with and cared for by another.

As Wayne Dyer says:

"Strong emotions such as passion and bliss are indications that you're connected to Spirit, or inspired,' if you will."

Our psychological state certainly influences our desire for pleasure and connection. So, if our lives are devoid of passion and meaning, or if we are living in fear, then our sexuality and sexual connections will be tainted with the same. If we become numb to life and disconnected from sources of joy, the fire within will surely go out.

It is then a sombre reflection on our modern lives that some 42 per cent of women suffer from sexual dysfunction, and Viagra continues to break records year after year[19]. These statistics show just how much life we have lost in our day-to-day and even the magical power of sex has been mauled by the mundane. It is surely sad that so many of us have to turn to medicine to support our sexuality. Although, in a way, it is not surprising. We are also taking antidepressants at an increasing rate and buying big on nutritional and anti-ageing supplements. In a world where we often act like robots, we are becoming reliant on medicines of all sorts to feel more human.

> *"It's difficult to have good sex on an empty heart or in ...a home without the spirit of abundant life."*[20]

A Lack of Desire

We are surrounded by media that warns any waning of sexual desire is cause for alarm bells. Frigidity is a sure sign of failure. A lack of sex drive is seen as a weakness. And yet, as suggested in the previous sections, there are many legitimate reasons why we may not desire intimate connection with ourselves or others.

We were born this way. Asexuality is a recognised sexual orientation. Just like people feel they were born gay, some people identify as asexual as they have no inherent desire for sexual activity with others.

Our hormones do not support a lively libido. We may be going through a period of hormonal flux, or our bodies may be flooded with the stress hormone cortisol. Either way, hormonal changes can negatively impact how much we feel like having intimate connections with others.

We have lost our spiritual spark. The extent to which you seek pleasure and connection can be a reflection of the amount of lust you have for life in general. Many of us endure days and nights in jobs we hate, spend hours in life-draining traffic, are weighted down with parental guilt, and then spend the weekends expending any shred of energy left on domestic chores. Our whole lives are set up to drain us of vitality, and yet we expect to suddenly find the spark of life when we snuggle up to our partner.

The problem with a lack of desire is not the lack of desire itself – it is our reaction to it. We always have the choice to:

- Approach the situation with compassion and care for ourselves as a whole person.
- Pathologize and pressure ourselves to get it fixed – to become more 'normal'.

The latter approach makes a person feel faulty, which only fosters fear. When operating in fear, a person is unable to give all of themselves. They shut down, exacerbating the problem they seek to solve. The only constructive approach is care and compassion.

Hypersexuality

On the other end of the spectrum, some people can have an incredibly high sex drive. There are those who have an intense and persistent preoccupation with sexual thoughts and behaviours. However, if this crosses the line to affect a person's wellbeing and daily life, it can be categorised as hypersexuality. Signs that desire has become problematic include:

- Excessive sexual thoughts: People with a high sex drive often have an abundance of sexual thoughts and fantasies. These thoughts can be intrusive and difficult to manage.
- Frequent masturbation: Frequent and compulsive masturbation is a common symptom. Individuals may engage in self-pleasure multiple times a day, sometimes to the detriment of other activities.
- Multiple sexual partners: People with a high sex drive may have a history of numerous sexual partners or engage in risky sexual behaviours.
- Excessive pornography use: Excessive consumption of pornography is a common behaviour associated with a high sex drive.
- Difficulty concentrating: The constant preoccupation with sexual thoughts can make it challenging to focus on daily tasks and responsibilities.
- Relationship strain: Hypersexuality can strain relationships, as partners may feel neglected or overwhelmed by their partner's sexual demands.

Similar to low levels of desire, hypersexuality can have physical and/or psychological causes.

Biological Factors: Some researchers believe that there may be a genetic or neurological basis for hypersexuality. Changes in brain chemistry and function could play a role in the intensity of sexual desire.

Hormonal Imbalances: Hormonal fluctuations, such as elevated levels of sex hormones like testosterone, can lead to increased sexual desire.

Psychological Factors: Certain psychological conditions, such as obsessive-compulsive disorder (OCD) or bipolar disorder, may be associated with hypersexuality. Trauma, childhood abuse, or early exposure to explicit sexual content may also contribute.

Medications: Some medications, particularly those affecting dopamine or serotonin levels (such as antidepressants), can impact sexual desire and may contribute to hypersexuality in some cases.

Substance Use: The use of drugs or alcohol can lower inhibitions and lead to increased sexual activity. Substance abuse may exacerbate hypersexuality.

Stress and Anxiety: High levels of stress and anxiety can sometimes manifest as a heightened sex drive as a way to cope with emotional discomfort.

Just like a lack of desire, a high sex drive is not inherently problematic or pathological. Many people have naturally high levels of sexual desire, and as long as it does not lead to distress or harm, it is not considered to be a cause for concern.

Desire, like gender, attraction, and pleasure, are inherently personal concepts. When we try to trap people into a box called "normal," we create anxiety that shuts down our ability to be authentic. The most important thing about desire is understanding what is true for you now, not what anyone else says you should be experiencing. Everyone is different—own and honour your uniqueness.

Nevertheless, if your level of desire is causing distress or interfering with daily life, seeking professional help from a therapist or healthcare provider is advisable. These people can help you understand the underlying causes and develop coping strategies that can help individuals manage and maintain a healthy balance in their sexual lives and foster respectful relationships.

The Difference Between Desire and Sexualisation

There can be a fine line between the desire for a connection with someone and the sexualisation of them. Understanding the distinctions between these concepts is important for fostering healthy relationships and respecting individuals.

Desire for a person encompasses a broader and more holistic form of attraction that includes emotional, intellectual, and physical aspects, all based on mutual consent and respect. It goes beyond physical appearance and includes a longing for intellectual and emotional intimacy, companionship, and a deeper connection. Desire denotes appreciation of the whole person, their personality, values, and unique qualities.

Sexualisation, however, involves emphasising a person's physical attributes and reducing them to sexual objects. It often neglects or ignores the individual's personality, thoughts, and emotions and places the primary emphasis on their sexual appeal. In sexualisation, any attraction or craving to be close to the person is driven purely by the desire to get in their pants!

Of course, as much as there have been great strides in consent education, we cannot control what other people are thinking about us. We cannot always tell if we are being sexualised, and so we cannot always contest or consent to it occurring. We do have much more control, though, over the sexualisation of ourselves. Self-sexualisation occurs when we only care about our physical aspects, over and above our mental, emotional and spiritual wellbeing. We strive to make ourselves as attractive as possible at the expense of our full potential. Success is being deemed desirable.

Unfortunately, social media is flooded with examples of self-sexualisation, with these influencers calling on others to keep up with the related trends. It is no coincidence that as concerns with the sexualisation of our children increase, so do the cases of body dysmorphia, loneliness and depression. It is not difficult to see how simplifying our lives to such superficial standards creates serious risks to our wellbeing.

Misreading Desire's Message

When people feel horny, usually their first thought is to seek out a Sexual Connection. They feel the need to act out sexually with themselves by masturbating or hooking up with someone else. However, you could be misinterpreting the message you are receiving from desire. You see, sexual feelings do not just indicate that you want to get intimate. Think about the function of sex – it is to connect and create. In this way, the urges you are feeling to get frisky may actually be calls to create something unique[21]. Yes, this creation may be through a merging of physical forms, but it could also be in any arena – in your work, the arts, in your home or with a community project.

Desire may be demanding new ideas and innovation, not just intimacy. It may be pushing you to put your ideas into action, to do something, develop something, produce a plan or piece of art, write a song or start a symphony, get started on a herb garden or help out at the local charity. It is easy to see sexual feelings simply as the need to get naked, whereas if you listen to their whispers, it may just be that they are asking you to follow your innate desire to create and contribute.

Pleasure

Sigmund Freud introduced the concept of the Pleasure Principle over a hundred years ago. Around 1900, he proposed that the Pleasure Principle is the innate drive that guides all human behaviour. It is the basic, instinctual drive that pushes us forward to find immediate gratification for our needs and desires. If desire is the longing you have to do something, then pleasure is the response you gain from doing it. Of course, our desires don't always end in pleasure. We may see an interesting act of intimacy in a film and fantasise about trying it. We actively pursue it and succeed in satisfying our curiosity. However, when we finally get to mimic the movie, it may not deliver any magic. Likewise, you may see a stranger at the other side of the bar who ticks all your attraction boxes, and at that moment your energy is sufficient to move into desire. You ask them to dance but leave disappointed. There was lust from afar but no pleasure within proximity. That is the thing with pleasure; you don't know until you try, and maybe even until you try it a few times.

There is also a feedback loop with pleasure. We remember those past experiences that have given up pleasure, and the happy hormones that resulted from the encounter. These pleasurable memories are filed away and become a source of future desires. Here is where Freud was correct – we will continue pursuing things that give us pleasure. It is a powerful motivator.

Fetish

The word fetish denotes a very particular source of pleasure. It is:

- Based upon a sexual interest or arousal.
- Associated with a specific object, body part, activity or scenario.

Fetishes can vary widely and may include items like specific items of clothing (for example, shoes or stockings), fabrics (for example, leather or velvet), specific body parts (for example, hands, breasts or feet), being treated like a child, dressed like an animal, having multiple lovers at the same time, or being restrained or spanked.

> *"And if I treat you like a child*
> *Will you let yourself go wild?"*
> *~ Madonna - Erotica*

There can be a lot of stigma and shame involved in having a fetish, especially if it is unusual or outside what others would consider decent. However, fetishes are a normal variation of human sexuality. Many people have specific preferences or interests that contribute to their sexual arousal. As long as these preferences are consensual and do not harm anyone involved, they are a healthy part of an individual's sexual identity.

It's also important to distinguish between a fetish and a fetish disorder. While fetishes are part of the rich tapestry of individual sexuality, a fetish disorder is a condition that requires intervention and support. With fetish disorders, the desires are unable to be satisfied without creating suffering either for themselves or others.

Desensitisation

There is an inevitable reality when it comes to pleasure and that is the desensitisation that occurs when you continue to receive it. Desensitisation manifests as a gradual reduction of enjoyment, and while disappointing, it is a natural process expected when a person is exposed to the same stimulus repeatedly over a prolonged period of time. For example, the joy you get when you first put on a new piece of clothing diminishes quickly with the fourth or fifth wear. And the excitement of the first kiss with a new partner will wane over the course of several weeks.

Unfortunately, desensitisation is often used as an excuse to detach from another person, with the reason given that "you just don't do it for me anymore." People must remember that this same desensitisation process will happen with the next person. It is just the way our brains are wired. Unless you are willing to look for deeper and more sustainable sources of joy, then you will continue to scrape the surface of superficial pleasure.

The dangers of desensitisation are evident when it comes to pornography. In the world of porn, variety, shock, and surprise are just one tap away. In just one click there is a new conquest, a new position, new punishments – the novelty is endless. The pleasure experienced releases huge amounts of dopamine, and with each click, the intensity continues. Like any other drug, over time, a point of tolerance is reached, and the feel-good reaction a person once got from watching porn subsides. This reduction in a pleasure reaction compels the person to watch more and more extreme porn to get the same kick. No longer is the person aroused by the same sexual adventures they once were. Not only does the sex drive wane, but this paves a path to porn addiction.

The desensitisation that porn presents also impacts intimate relationships. The fact is that a real person can never live up to the continual thrill that is presented with porn. Lovers look dull compared to the perfectly sculpted porn mistresses, and the desires of a normal human being pale to the limitless and extreme situations that the porn actors put themselves in. When a brain has become used to the high thrill of porn sex, anything real no longer becomes stimulating. The result is that a person can no longer get aroused when with a lover – men can't get it up, and women just can't get excited. The sexual dysfunction created by porn can take months to resolve. The disruption can also create a vicious cycle as people begin to feel broken, unworthy and ashamed and withdraw even more. People become dissatisfied with their intimate relationships and distressed when they cannot satisfy their lovers.

Self-Intimacy

The last part of the Sexual Self concentrates on the pleasure that we can deliver for ourselves. While some may focus on masturbation or self-sex, that is, stimulating your own genitals for pleasure, the concept of self-intimacy is much larger. It is about creating a personal and special relationship with this gift that is your body, a close connection and knowledge of the self. It is not just about the relief of tension or achieving the goal of orgasm. Sure, it can involve these things, but it can be broadened to include research into what makes us feel good and curious and what makes us feel afraid or unsafe. Self-intimacy is about knowing your curves and crevices, which bits feel tense and tight, and which sections are sensitive. It is about understanding those pieces of you that bring great pleasure and spark vulnerability.

Self-intimacy can be as simple as finding fabrics that feel great against your skin and treating yourself to these sensations. Or it could be experimenting alone with toys or props to see what emotions they bring up because self-intimacy is not merely about the physical. It is about gathering intelligence at every level - body, mind and spirit. Knowledge is power, and Self-Intimacy is about gaining knowledge about who you are and what you enjoy. Then, if the chance arises to connect with others, you already know your areas of comfort and risk. Self-Intimacy is done with the only person you can ever truly trust – yourself.

It is a pity that something as powerful as Self-Intimacy has been overshadowed by constrictive concentration on masturbation and the continued demonisation of this one deed. I suspect that most of us are living with generations of trauma around the idea of masturbation. Our ancestors in the 1600s were told it was a sin, and those in the 1800s were told that if you masturbated, you had an unbalanced mind. Your forebears would have been threatened with blindness, insanity and infertility if they sought their own pleasure. Even as late as 1936, Holt's Diseases of Infancy and Childhood recommended surgical removal or cauterisation of the clitoris as a cure for masturbation in girls. Boys were not spared through the traumas of surgical treatment for the mental disease of masturbation. The same effect was achieved through circumcision or sewing to shield the sensitive parts of the penis[22].

For hundreds of years, humans have feared masturbation. It may take many more until we fully appreciate that giving oneself pleasure is a fundamental and very special part of human sexuality. On this note, I would like to take this opportunity to thank Joycelyn Elders, the Surgeon General of the United States, who, in 1994, was forced to step down from her position for publicly asserting her belief that masturbation is natural and should be discussed in sexual education classes[23]. Thank you for your courage, Joycelyn, and your push for us to take another step forward in our search for understanding of our sexuality.

Elders was stating what has been evidenced since time immemorial: that while self-intimacy, in all its various forms, can be prohibited and punished, it does not mean that it has not been a normal part of sexual life for the whole of human history. Archaeologists have uncovered dildos in every age, as far back as classical Greek and Roman times. Even in the 1700s, they were openly sold in shops. In the 19th Century, self-intimacy was embedded into the erotica in the visual arts and literature.

We are now finally starting to make progress from centuries of prudishness. In 2015, Sweden gave us the word Klittra, meaning female masturbation. This term is a beautiful mix of clitoris and glitter, highlighting the role of the physical form for pleasure. A few years later, in 2018, the BBC even ran a TV show dedicated to showing people how to masturbate. Slowly, self-pleasure is being acknowledged as having a central place in our sexuality and as an important source of intelligence for understanding our personal sexual preferences. It is exciting to think that we are entering an era where creating a loving connection with your body is seen as beautiful.

Core Concepts

Attraction involves the gender identities, energies, physical forms, and personality traits that draw us to others.

What we find attractive is shaped by both our biology and cultural beauty influences.

Personality traits such as kindness, intelligence, and humour also contribute to attraction, reflecting our values and desires for connection.

Desire is the yearning to engage with something that attracts us, whether physical or emotional, and is influenced by hormones like testosterone, estrogen, and dopamine.

Desensitisation can reduce the enjoyment of repeated stimuli, particularly in cases like pornography, where continual novelty is sought at the expense of genuine connection.

Fetishes are specific sources of sexual pleasure tied to objects or scenarios. Fetishes are part of the rich tapestry of sexuality but can become disorders when they can only be met through causing distress.

Self-intimacy involves building a deep, personal relationship with one's body, going beyond masturbation to understand what brings pleasure, vulnerability, and comfort.

Chapter 6 – Sexual Fluidity

"Today, our sexuality is an open-ended personal project; it is part of who we are, an identity, and no longer merely something we do." ~ Esther Perel

It is well accepted that while much of our personality is stable over time, some elements shift and change as we work through more life challenges[24]. For example, major life events, such as marriage, parenthood, career changes, divorce, death of loved ones or other trauma, can influence personality development. These experiences may prompt individuals to reassess priorities, shift routines, and adopt new coping mechanisms. Also, cognitive abilities and emotional regulation tend to mature as individuals age, leading to changes in personality traits related to impulse control and emotional stability. Simply put, the characteristics that form our distinctive character change over time.

If we think about sexuality as a set of traits similar to our personality, then it is easy to understand that it, too, changes as we go through life. Sexual fluidity is the concept that an individual's sexual orientation, attractions, and desires can change over time and in different contexts. Unlike a fixed sexual orientation, sexual fluidity allows for a range of experiences and attractions that may not fit neatly into categories like heterosexual, homosexual, or bisexual. Sexual fluidity also does not imply a lack of authenticity or indecisiveness; rather, it acknowledges that sexual attraction can be dynamic and influenced by personal growth, relationships, and situational factors.

Recent research confirms that sexual fluidity is a common aspect of human sexuality, with most study participants experiencing at least one shift in sexual orientation across a decade. Numerous studies cite cases of individuals experiencing drastic changes in who they are attracted to, their levels of desire and what brings them pleasure. Sometimes, these shifts are transient, whereas, in other circumstances, they are long-lasting. For some, they occur in adolescence, for others, not until adulthood. And sometimes, these alterations are polar opposite to how the person defined themselves previously. Regardless, it has been shown that sexual fluidity is far more prevalent than we think.

Interestingly, some research suggests greater fluidity levels in women than in men. This finding is still being debated with further studies taking place to confirm this result. Nevertheless, while scientists may continue to test this claim, this idea does make sense to me. From my experience, there seems to be a lot less stigma about women forming bonds with other women than men sharing same-sex experiences. Therefore, while men may contemplate same-sex scenarios, they may be less likely to act on them; the social and psychological barriers to action may be too high. Women may not feel the same fear in embarking on experiments with another woman, expanding their capacity for fluidity.

However, this is only my uninformed view, and I look forward to the research results to identify what other physical, psychological or cultural factors may be at play.

The studies showing greater sexual fluidity in women also record that the shifts served a very distinct purpose – of broadening the woman's sexual experience. Over 80 per cent of those undertaking changes in sexual identity across the research period reported moving from a same-sex preference to a bi-sexual or unlabelled identity, which means they did not feel the need to categorise their sexual orientation. Only 16 per cent moved to a more limiting label of being heterosexual.

In contrast, it has been found that over time, men's sexual experiences become more narrow and specialised. Researchers have explained this as a consequence of women being able to gain great pleasure from both preferred and non-preferred partners. Whereas for men, the enjoyment with non-preferred partners is much less, reducing the likelihood of a repeat experience. If we apply the principle that we are all pleasure-seeking creatures, this explanation makes sense – women can go either way. However, I feel there may be more lurking below the surface of superficial stimulation, with factors such as stigma and shame possible contributors.

Regardless of gender, the research on sexual fluidity makes it clear that for some individuals, fixed constructs can never fully represent their openness to new experiences and their adaptability to specific situations, relationships, and self-concepts. The findings also make the argument for decreasing the use of rigid classifications for sexual identity even more relevant. Case studies provided by Lisa Diamond in the book *Sexual Fluidity* show the confusion and chaos that results when a person feels they are no longer living up to the expectations of their previous sexual preferences or fit within their original social group. They can feel fake or faulty when, in fact, all they are is flexible.

I think that the awareness, acknowledgement and acceptance of our sexual fluidity is fantastic and is a revelation that will relieve many. It takes a huge amount of pressure off what we believe we should be and allows us to focus on what is true for us at any point in time. This concept is especially important to discuss with your children. I have already had my 11-year-old daughter telling me that her school friend has decided she is lesbian. At this age, kids are already going through a tense time transitioning towards being teenagers. Now, it seems some also feel pressured to decide "what they are" and then label it and live by it. I worry when people place themselves into a box so early in life. Because in later years this personal identity may become a prison. It may not allow them to breathe and stunt their full becoming.

But by recognising sexual fluidity, we can give ourselves a break and remove the unhelpful barriers. We can flow with the forces within and around us and not fight against them, freeing up precious energy to invest in conscious and compassionate connections. When we appreciate our fluidity, we can live authentically across the ages and, in doing so, give our best selves in service to this world. As suggested by Fern Riddell though, what we have espoused as sexual fluidity may not be new, just a rediscovery of something long forgotten.

"We have pathologized sex to such an extreme that we have lost the understanding that it is something ever-changing. We have created specific communities – which have been necessary to pull together activists and fight for the rights of the majority within them. But these communities have also created rigid boundaries, defining who has the right to belong and who does not. Today, discussion surrounding gender or sexual fluidity is regarded as a unique moment in our sexual culture, when in reality it is closer to a return to the understanding of sex shared by our ancestors."[25]

Core Concepts

Sexuality is not fixed but can change over time.

Sexual fluidity refers to how sexual responses, including attraction, desire and pleasure, can shift, enabling a broader range of sexual experiences.

Research shows that most individuals experience some degree of sexual fluidity.

Women appear to have higher levels of sexual fluidity in men.

The aim of women's sexual fluidity is to broaden their range of experiences, with most moving to less restrictive sexual orientations.

In contrast, it has been found that over time, men's sexual experiences become more narrow and specialised.

Case studies reveal that fluidity can bring confusion when individuals feel they no longer align with their previous sexual preferences.

Awareness of fluidity is important for guiding younger generations, allowing them to explore their sexuality without the pressure of early self-labelling.

Sexual fluidity is not new; it is a rediscovery of ancient understandings of sex, suggesting a more natural, ever-changing nature to human sexuality.

Chapter 7 – Sexual Connection

"Sexuality is not about finding someone to make you whole, but about recognizing your own wholeness and choosing to share it with another."

It is through other people that we grow. And as much as our modern culture considers self-sufficiency a sign of success, meaningful relationships are essential to health and happiness. The work of Dr Richard Davidson and The Centre for Healthy Minds has shown connection is a key pillar of wellbeing, with connection being defined as:

A feeling of care and kinship toward other people, promoting supportive relationships and supportive interactions.

The skills related to connection in the *Healthy Minds Framework* include appreciation, kindness and compassion.

It is ironic that in a time where technology enables instant and continuous contact, loneliness has become one of the largest social issues. I believe loneliness has become such a concern because we mistake communication for connection.

Connection Requires Courage

Connection is not simply swapping selfies; it is opening oneself up to another, not just in body but in mind and spirit. Therefore, and this is the crux of connection, it requires vulnerability. It requires both parties to give and receive, touch and be touched, and let themselves be known.

"To be brave is to love someone unconditionally, without expecting anything in return. To just give. That takes courage because we don't want to fall on our faces or leave ourselves open to hurt." ~ Madonna

---

Therefore, creating a true connection is risky and requires courage, but the rewards are great. Without a connection with another, any intimate activities are merely superficial stimulation and could be considered mutual masturbation or payment-free prostitution.

"For as long as an individual uses a partner simply for the purpose of reducing tension, he really "masturbates on the partner," as our patients so often say. The mature individual's partnership moves on a human level. On the human level, I do not use another human being but I encounter him, which means that I fully recognise his humanness; and if I take another step by fully recognising beyond his humanness as a human being, his uniqueness as a person, it is even more than an encounter – what then takes place is love." ~ Viktor Frankl[26]

84

And while there is nothing wrong with enjoying passing pleasure, a life full of only facile friendships will likely leave one feeling very much alone. All of us need to feel known, understood, and appreciated. We all need to feel there is a place we belong. However, you don't achieve this without being open and authentic first.

What is most important in sexual connections, then, is not what form they take (with whom or how many, exclusively or open) but that they are created with consciousness and compassion.

Consciousness. Being aware of our needs, desires and boundaries and seeking to understand those of another. Consciousness also involves being alert to when we are challenged or triggered by the other and making clear and considered decisions about how we deal with the discomfort.

Compassion. Taking actions that reduce suffering for ourselves and others. Compassion is about acting with care for the wellbeing of all those involved.

Space for Individuality and Imagination

In the Sexuality Circle, there are four methods of making connections: talk, touch, creation and sex. However, there is also a great deal of space, showing that these are not the only ways you can form intimate connections. They are the most common and tangible, but there are also so many other activities that help you understand others and share their energy.

For example, simply sitting beside each other in silence is a beautiful way to tap into the person's traits, as is writing to each other or walking together. Being naked together in the daylight, even without touching, is an incredible act of intimacy that is often overlooked in the preoccupation to get physical. For some, falling asleep while still on the phone with the other person is special. There is no end to the things that can assist us in fusing body, mind and spirit. The only measures of success are the consciousness and compassion with which they are done and the learning that is gained along the way.

Talk

The words we use and the way they are spoken can either strengthen relationships or corrupt them through complacency and cruelty. That is why talking with another is a powerful part of building sexual connections and one often overlooked in the race to more physical pursuits. There is no doubt that building trust through talk and understanding what makes another person tick can be a terrific turn-on. More than just foreplay, though, it can create the foundation for a fun and fulfilling friendship.

"A lot of people are afraid to say what they want. That's why they don't get what they want." – Madonna.

Here are some ways talking can be used to foster fantastic Sexual Connections.

Compliments and positive affirmations. Expressing genuine admiration, appreciation and compliments can make another person feel good, boost their confidence and create a positive atmosphere, all conducive to creating a connection.

Building emotional intimacy. Engaging in meaningful conversations about emotions, feelings, and personal experiences can provide a great deal of intelligence about compatibility, enabling conscious decisions about progressing with the connection. Emotional intimacy can contribute to trust and enable deeper exploration and experimentation.

Expressing desires and preferences. Open and honest communication allows individuals to share their sexual desires, fantasies, and preferences. It can create a deeper understanding of each other's needs and compatibility and promote a safe, shared and satisfying space for experimentation.

Negotiating boundaries. Communicating about boundaries and confirming comfort and consent is essential for a healthy Sexual Connection. This activity involves discussing limits, checking in with each other, and ensuring everyone feels safe and respected.

Dirty talk. For some individuals, incorporating erotic or "dirty talk" during intimate moments can heighten arousal and create a more intense Sexual Connection. Establishing boundaries and ensuring that both partners are comfortable with this form of communication is important, as some people find it offensive. For some, it can bring up feelings of shame and guilt, introducing sinister shadows into the experience and shutting people down from fully engaging.

Learning together. Providing feedback, expressing pleasure, and communicating during sexual activities can enhance the overall experience. It helps partners understand each other's preferences and adjust their actions accordingly.

Dirty Talk as a Defence

It must be noted that while dirty talk can be used to create connections, it can also be a devious tool to defend against vulnerability. In the wonderful book *'Hold Onto Your Kids'*, Dr Gordon Neufeld and Gabor Mate explain how brazen talk about sexual activity is not necessarily brave. Sex without intimacy, just superficial screwing, is easy to talk about because there is no vulnerability involved. It is not transparent or courageous because it does not deal with the deep feelings involved in intimacy (or lack thereof), merely describing physical prowess and events. So, when someone shamelessly cites all of their sexual adventures, it may be a diversion from creating deep connections. Rattling off what they did distracts from how they felt, and this is what they may fear the most.

Words Hurt

Of course, using talk to create connections presupposes that each party is attentive and listening to the other person's verbal and non-verbal cues. Because there is nothing more destructive than feeling unheard, ignored or invalidated. This can happen when words are used to:

- Criticise – point out flaws for the purpose of boosting your own self-esteem or destroying that of the other person (or both).
- Blame – avoid or shift responsibility for one's actions.
- Stonewall – prevent other people from participating in discussions or refusing to participate oneself.
- Gaslight – manipulate or distort facts to make the other person doubt their own perceptions.
- Threaten – assert your power to the detriment of others.
- Humiliate – disparage another to embarrass them.
- Enflame negativity – focus only on the negative aspects to create an air of pessimism.
- Deceive – avoid or distort the truth to avoid responsibility, which destroys trust.
- Invalidate – dismiss or minimise another's experiences or feelings.

Touch

Touch is a powerful and effective way to create a Sexual Connection. It is a fundamental and intricate aspect of human interaction and elicits a myriad of physiological effects. When the skin receptors respond to tactile stimuli, neurochemical reactions are initiated. Positive touch, like gentle caresses or hugs, triggers the release of oxytocin, promoting feelings of trust and social connection, and reduces stress and anxiety levels. Additionally, touch stimulates the release of endorphins, the body's natural painkillers, contributing to an overall sense of wellbeing.

Furthermore, tactile interactions can lower cortisol levels, reducing stress and boosting our immune function. These physiological responses underscore touch's profound impact on human health, emphasising its role in fostering emotional bonds, reducing stress, and promoting overall physical and mental wellbeing. For this reason, touch is an integral part of forming connections not just physically but also in mind and spirit.

"Kiss me, I'm dying
Put your hand on my skin
I close my eyes
I need to make a connection." ~ Madonna – Skin

There are so many different forms of touch, each able to convey a range of various emotions. Here are some ways touch can contribute to creating a Sexual Connection.

Incorporating touch into communication. Physical touch can be integrated into verbal communication during intimate moments, reinforcing the connection between what is said and what is felt. A hand on the back when offering support or a touch to the cheek when expressing love makes the words even more meaningful.

Affectionate touch. Gentle, non-sexual touch, such as hugs, kisses, and cuddling, can create a sense of closeness and intimacy, laying the foundation for a deeper connection.

Expressive touch. Using touch to express emotions such as love, passion, or desire can deepen the emotional and sexual bond between partners.

Connecting through non-sexual touch. Engaging in non-sexual touch outside of intimate moments, such as holding hands or gentle touches throughout the day, can contribute to a continuous sense of connection.

Sensual touch. Delicate and purposeful touches that focus on pleasure and arousal can enhance the Sexual Connection. These may include caressing, stroking, or lightly tracing fingers over the skin.

Exploratory touch. Taking the time to explore each other's bodies respectfully and consensually can deepen the connection by fostering trust and vulnerability.

Playful touch. Incorporating playfulness, such as teasing touches or tickling, can create a light-hearted and fun atmosphere, enhancing the overall sexual experience.

Massage. Giving or receiving massages can be a sensual and relaxing way to connect physically. It provides an opportunity to focus on each other's bodies and offer a sense of calm and care.

Of course, clear communication about boundaries and obtaining consent before engaging in any form of touch is crucial. It ensures that both partners feel comfortable and respected. However, there is something even more important than consent, and that is the intention each party brings into the encounter. The selfish pursuit of pleasure will only grant temporal satisfaction. It is consciousness and compassion that are the foundations of fruitful and satisfying touch experiences.

While we have talked a lot about touching another person, it is also a wonderful way to build an intimate relationship with our surroundings. Spending time exploring all of the textures and energies in our environment can create a sense of closeness and belonging in the places we call home. Touching the ground and the trees and immersing yourself in the breeze or water is a wonderful way to feel a part of this planet and understand the interdependence of all things. In touching other people and other things, we are expanding our world and our experience and feeding back into spark and sustain our spirit.

Sex

As shown in figure two, in our modern world, there is an unbalanced focus on sex, to the detriment of understanding our overall sexuality. I do understand why. Sex is an extreme and, some might say, the epitome of pleasure, so it is natural there would be a preoccupation with the pinnacle. In my mind, though, concentrating on sex, rather than the completeness of our sexuality, is like fixating on the amount of money in your bank account while ignoring all the other assets (tangible and intangible) that create wealth. While cash-in-hand is an essential factor to consider in financial sustainability, it is only one small part of the overall picture, and distorted perspectives can be disastrous in the long run.

Because it is never just sex.

If sex were simply a physical act of procreation or pleasure, our lives would be simple. However, sex is never just sex. It is a notion and an act laden with enormous baggage. This baggage around sex has been handed to us from the adults who saw us through our formative years and added to by our own experiences. It is complicated by conflicting societal messaging around the meaning of sex and the signs of successful sexual connection.

Attracting a sexual partner, keeping them loyal and satisfying them sexually are all feats that society says make us successful, and so become an important metric in our evaluations of self-importance. Therefore, while we may like to think that sex is merely a physical act of pleasure or procreation, the human consciousness is far too complex. The vulnerability inherent in sex means that the tapestry of the physical union is inevitably interwoven with a plethora of deep physical, emotional and spiritual yearnings. Sex is inherently intermingled with our individual identities.

Some may argue that they can quite happily get their "rocks off" without a second thought. My question, then, is why were the rocks there in the first place? What luggage was the person hoping to offload through a sexual encounter? And suppose there is truly no consideration or concern for the welfare of the other after a casual encounter. In that case, I think you should probably be getting checked out for a severe case of narcissistic personality disorder. Instead, I think given the innate quality of empathy in humans, this may be more of an attempt at self-deceit and a narrative used to uphold naïve notions of independence and infallibility.

Some people may protest that there is something as simple as "just a shag" and that it does not have to mean anything. I disagree. Ending up in bed with someone means that, even for a moment, you were desired, and this comes with a sense of power. Any pleasure or pain gained from the experience also plants memories in the brain that influence your future behaviours and may be used to challenge or reinforce your beliefs about your own self-worth. The lead-up to the shag, the way it occurred, the resulting satisfaction, and the follow-up (or lack thereof) all contribute to the perceptions you have of yourself and other people. Sex always leaves some residue on our psyches.

Sex is a showcase for our loftiest aspirations and our deepest anxieties.

When Sex Subverts

For some, sex is used as a short-term distraction from days drenched in dealing with the cruel consequences of trauma and their insidious insecurities. Sex becomes a tool to gain a momentary sense of control and superiority. Specifically, sex can be used as a:

- Confirmation of self-worth.
- Weapon with which to wield power.

Securing self-worth

As suggested previously, the act of sex can be drenched in insecurity. In fact, I have heard it said that it is through sex that you get to truly witness your partner's neuroses. This is because, during sex, we expose ourselves and become vulnerable physically but also emotionally. We put our bodies in danger of injury, judgement and criticism. And even more profoundly, we risk rejection and the monstrous melancholy that comes with the thought that we are not worthy of being loved.

Being rejected as a potential sex partner can cut to the core of self-confidence. We begin to question our beauty, strength, and carnal desirability. In an instant, we are submerged into our deepest, darkest fear – of being unlovable and doomed to be alone. Our partner's sexual response becomes either a confirmation or denial of our value to them, the tribe, and society in general. With a lack of self-awareness and maturity, our partner's behaviour can instigate paranoia, suspicion, depression, withdrawal and mistrust.

The dilemma that arises from equating sex with self-worth is that when our sex lives change (as the laws of nature tell us they will), we can let fear creep in, use it to withdraw from the relationship and replace passion with self-protection. If this occurs, then the opportunity is missed to lean in and explore each other at a much deeper level. By allowing fear to pull us back, we do not get to peer into our deepest desires nor investigate structures and systems that keep us stuck. Wallowing in self-pity and floundering in failure becomes a convenient distraction to exploring our innermost worlds and finding those sources of worth that do not depend on the adoration of others.

Sex as a Source of Supremacy

Intimate relationships are often entered into to create a source of support and nurturing for each individual. However, they can also become a pure portrayal of Hegel's dialectic – two consciousnesses meet and begin a struggle for dominance. If one of the consciousnesses overpowers the other, then they enter into a master-slave relationship[27].

For the master, there can be a great thrill in asserting power through provision or denial of sexual favours or knowing that pleasure is yours to be taken at will. However, a relationship built upon seeking power over the other is surely no partnership. It does not matter whether we seek to exert power through the control of money, the adoration of offspring, sexual pleasure or brute strength. The result is the same. In relationships with a power imbalance, there is no longer a couple. Sex merely becomes a tool one party uses to assert their superiority, and the other uses to reinforce their lack of worth. Through immaturity, insecurity and the pursuit of influence, the bright colours possible through connection can be pulverised. They prevent the potential that sex has to transform and instead keep us stuck in second-rate soap operas.

The Potential of Sex

I have found no better guide on the potential of sex than Thomas Moore. In his book *The Soul of Sex*[28], he states that:

"In sex the soul has an unusually powerful opportunity to join body and spirit. Sex focuses our attention, as perhaps nothing else can, on our sensuous presence in this world and on another person, while at the same time it fulfills our desire for emotional and spiritual union with another, for

transcendence of our self-consciousness, and for meaningful experience. "

As this quote suggests, sex's eloquence can stir the couple to transcend the mundane and bring mystery and meaning into their lives. It allows them the space to step out of their worldly pursuits and mechanistic lives and to find the magic in their individual and intertwined bodies. It permits each to cast off clothes and concerns, open themselves completely, and be vulnerable and vibrant. In this way, sex becomes a ritual, celebrating each individual's vitality and the pleasure they co-create.

The reality is that while sex may not be as divine as described here, it is always transformative. It takes the colours brought by each individual and converts them into a work of art. The nature of the resulting artwork, though, depends completely on the consciousness contributed by each creator. And just as life is geared towards sex, our sexual creations then seep back into the threads of our everyday lives.

"If our sexuality is free of anxiety, everything in life may be comfortably creative, but if our sexuality is crude, then the whole of life suffers a parallel lack of refinement. "[29]

There is a circular relationship between the way we treat sex, our sexuality and our spiritual foundation, which will be explored further in the following chapter.

When Sex Wanes

No matter how evolved we may consider ourselves to be, we cannot escape our biology or the laws of nature. It is inevitable that we will see shifts in levels of sexual energy over time and that we may experience new sources of sexual stimulation. It is not that these situations occur that create problems for our relationship, but how we deal with them when they arise.

Some rampant romantics may want to change this title to 'if sex wanes' to suggest it is not a preordained predicament. But let's get real and view sexual desire like any other energy on this planet. As the law of rhythm tells us, it ebbs and flows. Like the tides, the seasons, and circadian rhythms – there is a flow and an oscillation to our lives. So, it is natural for there to be waves of sexual vibrancy and a push towards connection, and there will be lulls of withdrawal where celibacy and solace are needed. The outward movement of adventure and expedition will naturally seek to be balanced with the desire for retreat, contemplation and restoration of energy. And the deep desire to be embraced within a partnership will fluctuate with the fight to regain our individuality and independence.

It is not just the laws of nature that we have to deal with, but our biology. The hormones that have us lusting after our partner dwindle over time, making it harder to sustain sexual desire. There is no doubt also that the cortisol level generated by our busy lives would contribute to feelings of fatigue and fear, seconding sex as just another task to tick off the to-do list.

However, we are surrounded by media that warns any waning of sexual desire is cause for alarm bells. In our modern lives, where the measure of success is progress, not 'getting' sex is akin to failure. Moreover, suppose we equate the sexual responsiveness of our partner with our self-worth or sense of power. In that case, any rejection of sexual advances will automatically cause us to feel threatened, afraid, and unfulfilled.

If we expect sex as part of any relationship contract, then its lack of provision by our partner would also be viewed as a betrayal. For so many, sex is a symbol not only of attraction but of validation and acceptance. Being seen as a worthy mate is so entrenched in our psyche that rejection of sexual advances becomes automatically associated with the rejection of the entire person and an indication of their lack of value.

These insecurities have us leaping to unhelpful responses to sexual decline. They think where there is no sex, there is no attraction or love, and so there is no longer a true relationship. When sex wanes, it is common for one or both partners to withdraw and begin the process of self-protection, maybe even readying the psychological and emotional lifeboats.

But how often do the individuals isolate themselves instead of using this recess as an opportunity to dig deeper into each other? How often do they view it as a command to reassert control instead of a call to act compassionately to themselves and others? How often do they conjure visions of victimhood rather than see the chance to investigate the lack of verve? How easy is it for a person to slip into selfishness about the fact that they are not 'getting any' – whereas how much love does it take to contemplate that the other may be suffering through a loss of meaning, purpose and passion?

"Sex thrives in the air of friendship."[30]

Sex cannot be divorced from the life that drives it. Yet so readily, we see sexual dysfunction as a physical problem rather than a spiritual one. Sex represents vitality, so its suppression signals that we have lost our lust for life. Having and maintaining desire depends on having a life full of purpose and passion and supporting the other person to do the same. And so, spirituality and sexuality are inseparable.

Creation

"True sexuality is creative; it is an art, an expression, a flow. It's about connecting with life force, with joy, with vitality." — Shakti Gawain

What is also inseparable is sex and creation. It is interesting to know that in the system of chakras, sexuality and creativity are found in the same energy centre; they operate from the same energy source. And when you think about it, sex is ultimately a creative act, a merging of skills and energies to create personal pleasure and meaningful moments. However, sexual connection can also be found in many other forms of creation. For example, in painting a mural, co-parenting, preparing a meal, composing a song, running a business or renovating a house, a person shares their skills and hopes with another. Each participant in the creative process gets to better understand their own and other's intentions and insecurities, their natural way of working and their worries. In this way, joining in the act of creating something is a magical way to bring about a deep understanding of the self and the other and to strengthen sexual connections.

Core Concepts

Sexual connection requires openness, vulnerability, and a willingness to give and receive.

Loneliness in modern society is linked to mistaking communication for true connection.

Connection demands courage because it involves risk of rejection, but it is essential for deep and rewarding relationships.

Connection can be formed through various means— talk, touch, creation, sex, and through silent presence and simply sharing space.

Talk strengthens sexual connections by building emotional intimacy, expressing desires, negotiating boundaries, and fostering understanding and trust.

Touch is a powerful tool for connection, triggering positive neurochemical responses that promote trust, bonding, and stress relief.

Sex is never just sex; it is laden with emotional, psychological, and spiritual significance. Even casual encounters carry meaning and affect self-worth and identity.

The quality of the sexual connection depends on the individuals' intentions, the hopes and fears they bring into it and the level of vitality they have for life.

Chapter 8 – Sexuality and Spirituality

"Sexuality is the culmination of all that is beautiful about life, about energy, about vulnerability, and intimacy. It is an act of the body and the soul." — *Paulo Coelho*

Our sexuality is not a standalone entity. It is nourished by and feeds into a larger force I call spirituality. Understanding the relationship between our sexuality and spirituality empowers us, giving us a deeper understanding of ourselves and our place in the world.

What is Spirituality?

Given the deeply personal nature of both sexuality and spirituality, it's no surprise that a universally accepted definition is hard to come by. However, this diversity of perspectives makes these concepts rich and intriguing. Here's my take on spirituality, but remember, the beauty of it lies in its individual interpretation, giving you the freedom to define it in a way that resonates with you.

First, let's contemplate the notion of spirit.

Your spirit is the unique set of values, passions, and dreams you bring into this world and the distinct way you make these come alive each day.

So, for me, the spirit is not only about what you have but how you use it. There are so many people out there who have a passion for gardening, dance or volunteering. Still, each one will engage with it and express it in very different ways.

The word spirit may be troublesome for some people, so here are some other similar terms that you may be more comfortable with one of the following:

- Essence
- A sense of purpose
- Meaning
- The power within
- Innermost self
- Vibe
- Mojo
- Energy.

The thing about spirit is that there is not one part of my physical being in which it resides. It has not tangible boundaries. It is in all I am and all that I do. It not only delivers energy for what we need to do right now but calls us to be more, to develop, to learn and to grow. It holds us safely where we are but also encourages us to embrace this adventure called life.

Spirituality then, is the set of practices you use to sustain and express your spirit. Just as we care for our bodies, thoughts and emotions, spirituality is the process of investigating what is true for us, caring for our spirit and allowing it to live openly and fully.

Spirituality is more than just a concept; it's our sense of meaning and purpose in this world. It's what inspires us, motivates us, and gives our lives a deeper significance. And just like sexuality, spirituality has two main elements, one inward and one outward-looking:

1. **Being true to ourselves** means coming to know and connect with our authentic spirit, our internal sources of wisdom and power. It's about understanding our unique traits, values, and desires and living in a way that is true to these aspects of ourselves.
2. **Being true to something bigger than ourselves** means being aware of and uniting with a greater strength, be it in community, nature, or a higher power (such as God, the Universe or the Divine). It's about recognising that we are part of a larger whole and acting in ways that contribute positively to this collective entity.

So, both spirituality and sexuality have components within us and beyond us. They both have elements that represent our intrinsic and unique nature and become manifest when connected with something or someone outside ourselves.

Spirituality ≠ Religion

The word "religion" also has many variations in use. In this model, religion is a set of designated beliefs, behaviours, and practices. It is a doctrine delivered by an external source and founded upon the notion that someone or something has power over one's success and happiness.

Religion may or may not be a part of your spiritual circle. You may despise organised religion and so reject all external spiritual teachings. Alternatively, you may find great peace and inspiration in religions such as Christianity and Islam and honour the teachings in all you do. The point is people choose (consciously or otherwise) how much of their spiritual circle is taken up by external dogma and how much is taken up with their uniquely defined individual purpose. Some people may not subscribe to any religion and find their own way in the world. For others, all they know or have contemplated has been dictated to them by religious authorities. In this case, their religious circle takes up the whole spiritual space. There is no right or wrong when it comes to the element of religion. Each individual has their own level of awareness, motivation, intelligence and curiosity to bring to this element of their lives.

The Link Between Spirituality and Sexuality

There is an inextricable connection between our spirituality and our sexuality. Our fundamental beliefs about what is right and wrong and about our place in this world inform our thoughts about gender, attraction and pleasure. Our views about our life purpose also impinge upon our motivations and goals for intimate relationships. This connection also works the other way, as so beautifully put by Alice Walker:

"Sexuality Is one of the ways we become enlightened, actually, because it leads us to self-knowledge."

Sexuality is not just a means to get sex; it supports a deep knowledge of the self, which in turn can expand our awareness and lead us to enlightenment.

When you think of sex and spirituality, Tantra likely springs to mind. But Tantra is about much more than satisfying sex. It is a diverse and ancient spiritual and philosophical tradition. Tantra encompasses a wide range of practices, rituals, and teachings aimed at achieving spiritual growth, self-realisation, and union with the divine. Tantric sex is only practised after proficiency is gained in attaining relaxed awareness, ensuring that the practitioner is able to bring both consciousness and compassion to the Tantric connection. In this way, Tantra is part of a much broader spiritual practice rather than a sole tool for awesome sex.

Being True to You

At the core of our spiritual journey is the idea of being true to yourself. It's about aligning with who you are, not just in your actions and words but at a fundamental level. When you live authentically, you're not merely existing—you're thriving, connected to a sense of purpose and driven by values that matter to you. This section explores the key elements that help you understand and embody this authenticity: Purpose, Values, Religion, and Connection with your unique spirit.

Purpose: Why You Exist

Understanding your purpose is the first step to being true to yourself. Purpose isn't something external that someone hands to you; it's something you uncover through reflection and life experiences. It's the reason you get out of bed in the morning, the underlying motivation that drives your actions and choices. For some, their purpose may be rooted in making a positive impact in the world; for others, it may be about creating beauty, raising a family, or simply experiencing life to its fullest. Whatever it is, recognising your purpose gives meaning to your existence and provides clarity in navigating life's decisions. When you align your daily life with your purpose, you start living in a way that is authentic to you.

Values: What is Important to You

Values are the guiding principles that shape your behaviour and decisions. They reflect what truly matters to you, whether it's kindness, integrity, creativity, or independence. Being true to yourself means knowing your values and living in a way that honours them. It's easy to lose sight of your values in a world filled with noise, distractions, and societal pressures, but when you stay grounded in what is important to you, you can make decisions that resonate with your deepest self. Knowing your values acts like a compass, pointing you toward actions and relationships that support your authenticity.

Religion: Adoption of External Doctrines

For many, religion offers a framework of shared beliefs, practices, and values that guide their lives. It can provide a sense of belonging and a connection to something larger than oneself. However, it's important to recognise that being true to yourself within the context of religion means navigating these doctrines in a way that still honours your individuality. While adopting religious teachings can offer comfort and direction, reflecting on whether they align with your values and purpose is essential. If the doctrines support your authentic self, they can be powerful tools for spiritual growth. If not, it's okay to challenge or reframe them in a way that stays true to your spirit.

Connection with Your Unique Spirit

At the deepest level, being true to yourself means connecting with your unique spirit—the essence of who you are. It isn't about what society tells you to be or what external forces expect of you; it's about tuning in to your inner voice, the part of you that knows what feels right. Cultivating this connection requires quiet moments of reflection, time spent in nature, creative expression, or whatever activities help you feel most in touch with yourself. The more you nurture this connection, the more you can live authentically, in harmony with your true desires, values, and purpose.

Being True to Something Bigger Than You

"Life asks of every individual a contribution, and it is up to that individual to discover what it should be."
~ Viktor E Frankl

I believe the exploration of both our spirituality and our sexuality are endless pursuits. This is for two reasons:

Learning about sexuality and spirituality is a process that never ends. There is a big world out there of experiences. Each can be engaged and enjoyed intentionally to understand more about yourself. Every activity and interaction brings the opportunity to investigate those things that hurt and those that heal. Each moment provides the blessing to grow wisdom and compassion. The only limit to your understanding of the spirit is the extent to which you are committed to living with curiosity, an open heart and an open mind.

There is something bigger than yourself. Our call to spirit, our yearning to live true to our purpose, could be used for more than self-gratification. We desire to contribute to something or someone else, and we can use our gifts and energy toward making connections with and helping others. As Tony Robbins suggests:

"Only those who have learned the power of sincere and selfless contribution experience life's deepest joy: true fulfilment." ~ Tony Robbins

But I don't expect you to take Tony's word for the power of selfless contribution. Numerous scientific studies have proven the vital role of connection and contribution to our physical, mental, emotional, and spiritual health. In one of the most comprehensive studies, over 25,000 young adults from 58 countries were studied to identify the key contributors to wellbeing[31]. The researchers found intrinsic values such as meaningful social connections and community contribution were greater predictors of holistic health than extrinsic motivators such as power and financial gain.

The Ripple Effect

We were born with unique perspectives and abilities that can enrich our own lives. But we were also born with the ability to use them to improve this world. Our potential to contribute to our communities does not mean that we all must become activists fighting to save the planet or volunteers on the front lines of human distress. While these are noble pursuits, being true to something bigger than yourself ultimately begins with yourself. The changes you make to be true to yourself can gently ripple outwards.

In the book *Active Hope*[32], Macy and Johnstone outline four levels of community through which the ripple of our spirit can travel.

Figure 5 - The Four Levels of Community

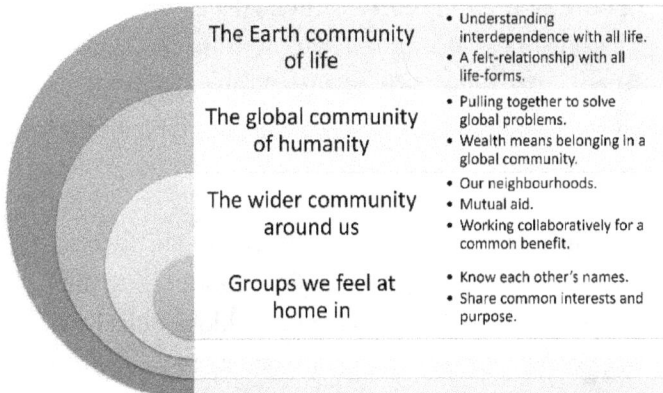

The Earth community of life	• Understanding interdependence with all life. • A felt-relationship with all life-forms.
The global community of humanity	• Pulling together to solve global problems. • Wealth means belonging in a global community.
The wider community around us	• Our neighbourhoods. • Mutual aid. • Working collaboratively for a common benefit.
Groups we feel at home in	• Know each other's names. • Share common interests and purpose.

Adapted from Macy, J., & Johnstone, C. (2012). *Active Hope: How to Face the Mess We're in without Going Crazy* (5&06&9th ed.). New World Library.

Groups we feel at home in. These are our family groups, religious groups or interest groups. In these communities, you know others by name and share similar values and goals.

The wider community. This level includes the broader communities that we associate with and join with to support each other. These include our neighbourhoods, suburbs and even country communities. It also includes membership and volunteer groups where we combine resources for a common cause.

The global community of humanity. Beyond our neighbourhoods, countries, and clubs in the broader community of all humans. At this level, we strive to solve problems that affect all of us no matter where we live, our race, religion, age, gender or sexual affiliation. By being born into this life as a human, we are all automatically part of the global community of humanity, with the capacity to better the lives of our brothers and sisters across the world.

The Earth community of life. At this level, we recognise that all life is interdependent, be it on the land, oceans, or skies. We think beyond just the wellbeing of the human species and consider how we can contribute to the health of all beings.

As the diagram shows, the work we do to bring greater consciousness and compassion to our sexuality ripples outwards. When we understand and love ourselves, we have a greater propensity to establish strong and supportive Sexual Connections. These positive relationships then impact your family and social circles and create role models for what is possible in your broader community. Your maturity and care will inspire others to do their own work and thus begin a wave of goodwill that ripples out into the world. This is why Mahatma Gandhi said:

"Be the change that you wish to see in the world."

Core Concepts

Sexuality and spirituality are deeply connected and nourish one another. Both are central to understanding ourselves and our place in the world.

Spirituality is personal and encompasses our sense of meaning, purpose, and connection to something larger than ourselves. It has both inward and outward elements—being true to ourselves and aligning with something beyond us (e.g., community, nature, or a higher power).

Spirituality is not the same as religion; while religion offers structured beliefs and practices, spirituality can exist independently or alongside it, depending on individual preferences and experiences.

Being true to yourself means aligning with your values life purpose. Living authentically brings deeper satisfaction and harmony.

Being true to something bigger than yourself recognises that we are part of a larger whole and can contribute positively to the world through our unique gifts and strengths.

The ripple effect of living authentically extends beyond oneself, influencing various levels of community—from close family to the global and Earth communities.

Spiritual and sexual exploration are ongoing and limitless. Every experience offers a chance to grow in consciousness and compassion.

Chapter 9 – Sexual Materialism

In our modern world, materialism has become a dominant force, shaping how we live, think, and even how we approach our sexuality. Just as Chögyam Trungpa warned about the dangers of spiritual materialism in the 1970s, we now face a similar challenge with sexual materialism—where our bodies, desires, and intimate relationships are often treated as commodities to acquire status and external validation. It is crucial to consider sexual materialism when seeking to understand our sexuality because it distorts our connection to ourselves and others, reducing sexuality to a transaction rather than a profound expression of identity and human connection. By examining the ways materialism influences our sexual lives, we can begin to reclaim our authenticity and create more meaningful, enriching connections.

The Recognition of Spiritual Materialism

In 1973, Chögyam Trungpa wrote the confronting text *Cutting Through Spiritual Materialism*[33]. He saw Eastern religions such as Buddhism becoming increasingly popular in Western countries but being adopted with superficial and inferior intentions. He saw converts grasping spirituality as a solid construct, seeking to own, improve, display it to the world and use it for their sense of self-worth. Almost 50 years later, his words ring true for the physical manifestation of our spirituality—our sexuality.

What Is Materialism?

Materialism is defined as a value system preoccupied with material possessions and the social image they project. It places overwhelming importance on physical objects and believes that these, and their inherent statements about identity, are the most important things in life. I posit that materialism has become the religion of the modern world. Materialism fits the definition of a religion in that it is:

A set of beliefs, behaviours and practices. Materialists believe that the right phone, shirt, car, skincare product or spouse will make them happy and show success. So, they watch people who appear successful and happy, find out what phone, shirt, care or skincare they use, what kind of spouse they have, and then set about replicating these possessions in their lives.

An externally driven dogma. These beliefs and behaviours are founded on the prime concern about what others think of you. They are based on you being seen to have and to be doing the right things. A person's sense of worth is established through the objects and activities that denote success, being merely the superficial layer of their full existence.

Ultimately, materialism is based on fear—the fear of never having enough, never being enough, of being ridiculed and rejected. It is also a clear indicator of insecurity. When a person does not feel that they are inherently worthy, they will continually try to cover over who they are with tangible things that indicate success.

And while we all like to think of ourselves as strong and independent adults, there are gods in this religion dictating standards of what makes a great life. These gods disguise themselves as marketers and politicians. Marketers manipulate your greatest fears and your deepest desires to make you buy stuff. Politicians pull the policy strings to ensure all the economic indicators are moving in their favour — employment, GDP, business confidence, and consumer spending. Growth is good, and growth is fuelled by people buying stuff! Growth will get them re-elected and preserve their power.

Don't get me wrong; if anyone wanted to give me a trinket from Tiffany & Co. or an auto from Audi, I would quite happily take it! I like beautiful things just as much as the next YouTube Influencer. Appreciating and celebrating magnificence is life-affirming, whatever the object may be. The danger comes when appearance and possessions turn inwards and begin to define your sense of identity and worth. With the religion of materialism, what you have becomes more important than who you are. The true, full and beautiful you tend to get lost in the fuss around maintaining facades. The dangers of a materialistic preoccupation are real and were foretold by the 18th Century poet Lucien Jacque:

"Humans are nourished by the invisible. We are nourished by that which is beyond the personal. We die by preferring its opposite." ~ Lucien Jacque

Materialism creates death and destruction in all aspects of our lives. It reduces our sense of security[34] and the attention we have to place on our relationships. The research shows that when materialistic values increase, life satisfaction, self-image and contentment with romantic relationships decrease[35]. People are also more likely to pay for cosmetic surgery when they place the greatest importance on the tangible and material appearance of things, especially themselves.

Moreover, rather than having us feel part of a tribe, materialism breeds a sense of loneliness and isolation. This loneliness promotes even more consumption as more things are sought to fill the emotional void[36]. It seems that being a material girl (or a material boy) is a sure way to end up sad, anxious, and alone.

You will never be content when your sense of purpose is rooted in having stuff, because, as we all are well aware, there is always something new to surpass what we already have. In this way, when you are a materialist, your life is driven by getting the things you should have or becoming what you should be. You lose your sense of autonomy and an individual sense of purpose. You lose your ability to understand and share your unique gifts with the world because you are constantly distracted by securing other people's favourable opinions.

More than the impact on the individual, materialists are not activating the important second element of spirituality — being true to something bigger than yourself — and so are sacrificing their great contribution to a broader community. Whether it be their family, neighbours, profession, humanity or all creatures on the earth, they all lose out because the materialist is obsessed with their aims for possession. This loss of greater meaning is devastating and is shown in the continual increase of violence, addiction, depression, and our planet's destruction.

"We are enriched not by what we possess, but by what we can do without." – Immanuel Kant.

The Heart of Sexual Materialism

Now, we get to the juicy bit. If you are willing to agree that the modern religion is materialism, then for most people, their driving purpose is material success, with all of the associated trappings of tangible goods and acknowledged identity. Their values revolve around possessing the "best things" and having the "right" appearance. They are fundamentally afraid and insecure but plaster these doubts over with possessions — of goods and identities. So, it is inevitable that these values and behaviours will feed into how they understand and express their sexuality.

The following list describes what sexual materialism looks like:

- People will not define their own gender identity or energy — they will have it defined for them by what is trending on TikTok that day.
- People will not be true to what they feel is attractive — they will be driven by what they are told is hot.
- People will aim to own the best labels (sexy, tight, thick, smokin') and seek to rid themselves of the

inferior labels (slut, whore, loose, cheap, nasty, skinny, wanker).

- There will be a desire to have the best boobs, butt or biceps possible and work to acquire the "right" partner.
- Concerning pleasure, people will turn to the sex marketplace to define this for them — allowing porn in all its forms to dictate what they should enjoy.
- When it comes to intimate connections, they will focus on the most tangible of artefacts — sex. Other people's desire to have sex with them will signify their level of worth in the world.
- Sex becomes a commodity sold with a promise of status, pleasure, success and happiness. It is something to get, not something to share.

Sexual materialism, then, is how a materialistic philosophy is played out through our sexuality. It is a state of mind that believes our sexuality and intimate connections are there to relieve us from superficial suffering and bring us nothing but happiness. Instead of our sexuality enabling greater self-knowledge and a connection to our higher selves, we possess and use it to gain recognition and acceptance and as a yardstick of success. And instead of our sexuality enabling full, mutual and meaningful connections with others, it turns others into achievements and trophies.

We are given this amazing life and a wealth of gifts to share with the world. We have the opportunity to look deep within, understand our true and unique selves, and, through our bodies and relationships, share our matchless spirit with others. We can appreciate the openness of our femininity or the drive of our masculinity and use this to love ourselves and others honestly. We can treasure what brings us pleasure and use this to celebrate life and cultivate pure joy. We can feel our desire and use this to create things that respect, unite and elevate. But these opportunities are lost if we focus on the superficial and tangible aspects of our lives. The things that truly sustain us — being true to ourselves and something greater than ourselves — are lost, and so is the chance to grow into our incredible potential.

Why We Get Sucked into Sexual Materialism

"We are at a seminal moment in our sexual culture. Our modern sexual lives have become geared solely towards our own individual experience, and the emphasis on sex as shared pleasure – something that was so important to our ancestors – is being erased. We see the evidence for this in every aspect of our culture, from songs to films, to self-expression. But how has this happened? Why are we so keen to abandon the messages and beliefs of the past that advocated kindness, consent and sexual harmony in favour of selfish loneliness?" ~ Fern Riddell[37]

Our sexuality is an incredibly powerful resource, but the pull of materialism is pussifying it. While we are distracted with our busy lives, it is stolen, smashed, mangled and sullied, and then sold back to us in pretty packaging at an exorbitant profit. It is not just our debt levels that are suffering as a result. The preoccupation with sexual materialism is repressing our whole human evolution.

Why do we allow this to happen? Why have we let sexual materialism become the norm? We have seen how destructive materialism is. So why are we letting our children follow this painful path and let their bodies and relationships become part of the global sexual marketplace? I believe there are three main reasons:

1. We have allowed marketers to distract us away from the meaningful and towards the superficial.
2. We have been duped into forgetting spirituality and its life-sustaining power — perhaps because we confuse it with the concept of religion. Or perhaps we think we have become so smart that we no longer need spirituality?
3. We have been sucked into the entertainment of social media and lost the courage to talk openly about the core aspects of our humanity, for example, sexuality.

The void created by these occurrences has allowed those preying on fear and insecurity to march straight in unchallenged.

The Solution

As Missy Jubilee says in her film *Weapons:*

"It's never good stuff that fills a vacuum."[38]

And in this case, her wise words ring true.

It is time to get brave and recognise that we are spiritual creatures and that by ignoring the spiritual dimension of sexuality, we are creating suffering. We must push back against those seeking to profit off our power and reclaim the privilege of our sacred sexuality.

Core Concepts

Materialism operates like a religion, defining identity and self-worth through possessions and appearances. It is a religion driven by fear and insecurity.

Materialism disconnects us from our true identity and distracts us from fostering meaningful relationships.

Sexual materialism reduces sexuality to a commodity for status and external validation, prioritising superficial achievements and identities over individual authenticity and meaningful connections.

In sexual materialism, the components of our sexuality are shaped by market forces, with people looking to trends to help them define their gender, what they find attractive and what successful sex looks like.

Within sexual materialism, sex becomes a commodity, used to gain status rather than create genuine connections and self-knowledge.

Spirituality and sexuality are intertwined, and neglecting this connection leads to shallow experiences and a loss of self-awareness.

Reclaiming our sexuality involves removing the deep influence of profiteers, embracing its spiritual dimension and learning to deal with vulnerability rather than plaster over it with possessions.

Chapter 10 – Sexuality and Maturity

"Maturity is the discipline of giving up and giving away, to see what is left and what is real." ~ David Whyte[39]

Our sexuality is intricately linked to our spirituality, which encompasses our beliefs, sense of purpose, and desired contribution to the world. However, both our spirituality and sexuality are influenced by our level of maturity. Therefore, understanding the process of adult development, our current position and its potential impact on our Sexual Self and Sexual Connections is crucial. This introspection can lead to a greater awareness of ourselves and how we work within relationships, and empower us to take control of our personal growth.

According to Dr Kegan, The Theory of Adult Development[40] has five stages, summarised in the table on the following page.

The stages most relevant to the discussion of sexuality are two to five. These stages present maturity as a shift from reliance on others' opinions to an independent sense of self.

Figure 6 - The Five Stages of Adult Development

Dr. Robert Kegan's Theory of Adult Development			
Stage	**Stage Name**	**Characteristics**	**Where Found**
Stage 1	**Impulsive Mind**		Early childhood.
Stage 2	**Imperial Mind**	• It's all about my needs • I will follow norms and trends to get rewards and avoid punishment	Adolescence and 6% of the adult population.
Stage 3	**Socialised Mind**	• It's all about what you think of me • I seek out and depend upon external validation. • I am defined by others.	58% of the adult population.
Stage 4	**Self-Authoring Mind**	• It's all about what I think of myself. • I take responsibility for my own opinions and actions. • I have the power to create the life that I want.	35% of the adult population.
Stage 5	**Self-Transforming Mind**	• I release myself from expectations around my identity. • I am free to question, challenge, expand and reinvent myself.	1% of the adult population.

The Imperial Mind — It's All About Me

While mostly a feature of adolescence, the Imperial Mind is still found in approximately six per cent of the population. Suppose you line up one hundred people. In that case, you can expect that around six will consider that life is all about them. Everyone else is there to meet their needs and wants, so relationships become transactions.

Decisions around attraction, desire, pleasure and partners are based on their perceptions of external punishments or rewards, with the ultimate choice being based on which path delivers the most personal benefit. If the person wants safety and security, they will make decisions in line with the culture of the context in which they live. If they seek notoriety through rebellion, then their decisions will be based on bucking social norms. Either way, choices about their sexuality or how they enact it will depend on what they will get out of it.

The Socialised Mind — It's All About What You Think of Me

In Stage Three, the Socialised Mind, our concerns move away from our needs to how others experience us. We take on external thoughts and beliefs as our own and allow ourselves to be defined by our family, society, ideology, or culture. We become preoccupied with how others see us and even go further to transfer the views of others onto ourselves. When a person is operating from the Socialised Mind, they don't have a strong sense of an independent self and so continually seek out external validation for a sense of self. In this stage of development, the moral foundations of authority and loyalty are key, whether that be loyalty to social conventions or the person's partner or peer group.

The Socialised Mind stage usually occurs when we break away from our families and begin our adult lives but still have a substantial need for attachment. Separating from parents can be scary, so we spend our lives finding someone who will possess us, care for us, and provide a refuge from the storms of life. We do this by being like the people we want to be a part of.

For people stuck in the Socialised Mind, Sexual Connection is a key tool to confirm that:

"We do exist and are worthy of love. We exist and are meaningful because we are a part of someone else."[41]

So, it is in this stage that we are most likely to see sex being subverted to reinforce our sense of self-worth and turned into a possession to secure favourable opinions from others.

It is interesting to see that over half (58 per cent) of the adult population lives with a Socialised Mind and spends time trying to live up to the expectations of others. Out of every hundred people, almost 60 seek their identity through relationships with others and conformance with social conventions.

In my research, I asked separated and divorced people what led them to get married in the first place. The major reasons were:

- To be normal.
- It was expected.
- It was just the next logical step in the relationship.
- To make my parents happy.
- Everyone else was doing it — I didn't want to be left behind.

These responses show clearly how much the Socialised Mind contributes to our choices around Sexual Connections. Most of us commit to sexual exclusivity not necessarily because it is natural, not because it is best for our partner or us, but because we are insecure and desperate to fit into the tribe.

When a person is operating with a Socialised Mind, there are two real dangers, being:

1. The withholding of vulnerabilities.
2. That they will live divergent lives.

Fear of what the other person thinks about you results in repression. We withhold the parts of ourselves we think others will not like and hide our vulnerabilities for fear of ridicule or rejection. We hide not only from other people but also ourselves.

"Nothing is easier than self-deceit." ~ *Demosthenes*

We can easily convince ourselves that the stories we tell are true. Still, all deception ends in distress, for we face the reality slap sooner or later. The way reality wakes us up can take the form of either being found out to be a fraud or the nagging feeling that you don't fit in. Only by sharing our vulnerabilities can we create constructive connections based on trust. Otherwise, if the opportunity for trust is not afforded, there will always be doubt about whether the person can live up to our hopes and a continual concern about being rejected.

The other danger is that the parts we have put on or exaggerated to impress become the backbone of our relationship. What happens when the fake parts become the ones that the other person comes to love? This situation results in cognitive dissonance, and then we only have two choices to solve the conflict:

- Exit the relationship and start again by being more authentic.
- Change our values to align with the persona we have portrayed and others have bought into.

Living our lives by social norms and the expectations of others may provide short-term comfort, but inevitably is vexing. It creates conflicts and dilemmas between our thoughts and the fears inherent in non-compliance. It puts us in defensive mode and creates connections imbued with insecurity.

Yet, we place our lives on social media platforms, which significantly shape our perceptions and trap us in a dependent state. Social media can reinforce the Socialised Mind by promoting conformity and discouraging individuality. It can do this by:

- Making divergence from norms or trends public, increasing the likelihood of criticism, and thus reducing the likelihood of individuality.
- Reinforcing the incorrect notion that sexuality = sex and sex = porn and that these are the standards by which all sexual connections should be judged.

Despite the dangers of this stage of development, it is an essential period of growth. A child must know what it is like to be subsumed before learning to be separate. They must first know the support of the tribe to find the strength to step outside of it. They must feel the frustration at the confines of convention before they are motivated to take action to crack them. They must know what it is like to be part of a group to know also what it feels like to be an individual. The problem is not that this stage of development exists, but when people get stuck within it and bring the downsides of it into their connections. Allowing others to tell us what is important is a sure way to continually be dissatisfied and spend our days chasing an unrealistic ideal. Seeking external validation for ourselves also means we distort our precious individuality and deny sharing it with those we profess to love. Withholding the self is ultimately a deep self-repudiation and a sign of distrust in the other.

The Self-Authoring Mind — It's All About What I Think of Myself

It is a big leap from the Socialised Mind to the Self-Authoring Mind. It takes a huge amount of courage to ignore the pull of external expectations, define our sense of identity and our unique sexuality and find our own sustainable sense of self-worth. It is an incredible responsibility and a massive risk, yet one that holds great rewards. The blessings that come with a Self-Authoring Mind include the freedom from being trapped by others and moving in directions aligned with our values. We no longer need to gain the approval of others but come to have confidence in our own counsel, authority and voice.

Most importantly, at this stage, we recognise ourselves as an ever-changing being. We appreciate that we are not fixed in body or mind and have the power to create the life we want. We make decisions based on what is important to us, not what is important to friends, family or society.

Concerning Sexual Connection, what is exciting at this stage is that we can make decisions fully and freely. And we have a strong sense of independence and self-worth that we bring into creating more balanced and equitable relationships. We deeply understand and connect with ourselves, enabling us to understand and connect with others. And importantly, we build a personal intimacy that provides a helpful counterbalance to the pull of becoming lost in a couple. We no longer seek merging or union but look to appreciate and celebrate differences.

"The better differentiated she becomes, the more she is able to mix with others without losing her sense of self."[42]

In his theory of Motivation and Personality[43], A.H. Maslow also suggests that this increasing maturity allows us to appreciate and accept the dichotomies within ourselves. Because opposites are always present. We tend to see them as contradictions and judge them harshly. However, in this stage of maturity, we come closer to knowing the truth that both sides of the coin are ever-present. We can acknowledge that there are times when we are lonely and need someone and that there are times when we don't. We can acknowledge that there are parts of us that are yearning for acceptance by the tribe and parts of us that are desperate to escape it. Our maturity allows us to be kind to ourselves for the conditioning that has brought us here and compassionate enough to allow ourselves to forge a new path. Maturity is about building "integrative functioning" skills[44] and the ability to reconcile the ever-present dichotomies of rebellion and rejection, comfort and compliance.

The Self-Transforming Mind

Stage Five, the Self-Transforming Mind, moves beyond appreciation and empowerment of our identities to the complete release of expectations around who we are. With this level of maturity, we understand that our lives are complex, and so are we. We know that we are continually changing and allow ourselves to expand and reinvent ourselves to take on new challenges. While we were willing to question social conventions in the previous stage, in Stage Five, we are also ready to question ourselves. We are open to seeing ourselves from different perspectives.

David Whyte describes this magic of maturity as follows:

"But maturity beckons also, asking us to be larger, more fluid, more elemental, less cornered, less unilateral."[45]

With so few examples among the population, it is challenging to have a concrete idea of the consequences of operating from a Self-Transforming Mind. I can only theorise that at this stage of maturity, people no longer self-label into any categories. I suspect they don't even burden themselves with forming an identity. Their relationships and actions are driven by growth values and the pursuit of living up to their full potential. One could imagine, too, that they are driven to assist others to do the same. They do what is right and true for them, knowing they will evolve over time and without the conflict that the rest of us feel about change. In the Self-Transforming Mind, the person is truly independent — even of their own expectations. They can live in the magic of who they are in each moment.

Germaine Greer seems to be describing this stage of maturity in the following passage from *The Female Eunuch*.

"The essential factor in self-realisation is independence, resistance to enculturation; the danger inherent in this is that of excessive independence or downright eccentricity; nevertheless, such people are more capable of giving love, if

what Rogers said of love is to be believed that 'we can love a person only to the extent that we are not threatened by him'.

Our self-realising person might claim to be capable of loving everybody because he cannot be threatened by anybody. Of course, circumstances will limit the possibility of his loving everybody, but it would certainly be a fluke if such a character were to remain completely monogamous."[46]

Here, Greer suggests that the freedom that comes with the Stage of the Self-Transforming Mind makes it unlikely that a limit would be placed on loving just one person. She proposes that monogamy becomes less relevant as a person matures and has the ability to rest in self-confidence and fully appreciate the totality of another person.

Some may use this submission as evidence that those in polyamorous relationships are more self-transforming and superior to their socialised-mind counterparts. However, the experience of my somatic psychotherapist would suggest otherwise. She has found the counselling work with polyamorous participants to be some of the most distressing and difficult of her career. She has found that many people participate in polyamorous relationships to prevent the need for personal growth. This form of relationship provides ample opportunity to avoid and distract from deep inner work.

Moreover, the neuroses that a person into a partnership can be multiplied with each additional member of the party. Therefore, the extent to which polyamorous relationships will be helpful and healthy depends upon the maturity of the individuals residing within them. In this way, they are no different from monogamy, which also relies upon respect and personal responsibility to allow the participants to flourish.

Nevertheless, the increased freedom that seems to come with advancing maturity sounds very similar to the notion of sexual fluidity. For this reason, it would be interesting if future studies on sexuality fluidity include investigations into the participants' level of maturity to determine whether this developmental variable impacts the propensity to alter desires over time.

Maturity ≠ age

As noted by Dr Gordon Neufeld,

> *"Physical growth and adult physiological functioning are not automatically accompanied by psychological and emotional maturation."*[47]

While there is some correlation between age and stage of development, this is only sometimes the case. The majority of people may travel along the stages as they get older. Still, there will always be those operating from a stage in direct contrast to their age. People can still be operating like imperialists well into and past middle age. And some enlightened teenagers can surprise us with their flexibility and freedom from a fixed identity.

Given the general progression through the stages, it is understandable that it is around middle age that most people begin to question the notion of traditional relationships and the suitability of sexual exclusivity. This questioning could be caused by their troubled experiences of marriage and monogamy or increased recognition of the complexity of human needs and desires. Or perhaps they have felt the dissatisfaction from denying their individuality and now feel the push from the moral foundations of authority and loyalty to the foundations of liberty and care.

Whatever the reason, it is not surprising to see these more seasoned life travellers showing up on adultery, dating or sugar daddy sites, eager to explore parts of their sexuality they may have chosen to repress in their conventional relationships.

How Do You Grow Up?

One of children's most annoying yet admirable traits is their continual questioning. Asking "why" is an indicator of curiosity to be celebrated and an indispensable contributor to individuality.

"Courage doesn't happen when you have all the answers. It happens when you are ready to face the questions you have been avoiding your whole life." ~ *Shannon L. Alder*

To progress along the stages of maturity, you must take on the responsibility of asking questions. Courage is required to not only ask the questions but also to answer the questions honestly and to be open to the fact that you may not like some of the responses that arise. We cannot rejoice in the truth (as love does) without first being willing to hear it.

"Just as surely as distress must follow self-deceit, healing must follow self-honesty." ~ Vernon Howard

---

There are so many questions that could be relevant to the understanding of your sexuality, but here are a few thought-starters:

- What level of maturity am I currently at?
- How is this level of maturity shaping my Sexual Self and my Sexual Connections?
- How have other people's opinions shaped my beliefs about my sexuality? Are there ones I disagree with but follow along with anyway?
- What about my sexuality scares me, and how does this fear inhibit my growth?
- How much do I feel like I am more concerned with being normal rather than what is natural for me?
- What would I like to understand more about my Sexual Self?
- How much do I feel like my Sexual Connections to date have been based on fear rather than love?

The Role of Maturity in Sexual Connections

I have learnt the hard way that sometimes you must spend decades digging through the grime of who we aren't to find the gem of who we truly are. Through our self-development, we also expand our capability to create nurturing and evolving connections. Then and only then can we express and share this wonderful gift of ourselves fully and freely, and find a place where we truly belong.

"Individuality, on the other hand, is the foundation of true community because only authentically mature individuals can fully cooperate in a way that respects and celebrates the uniqueness of others."[48]

This way, our maturity (or lack thereof) can hinder or help create conscious and compassionate connections. The interactions of two immature individuals are fraught with fear and founded upon facades. Soon or later, external agitations or internal tremors will threaten the structure tenuously held and likely bring the relationship down. The individuals are left dazed, confused, and alone to sort through the rubble.

Suppose we want connections that enable ourselves and the other to flourish. In that case, I first need to be well on the path to my independence. To prosper within a pair, a person must first be able to celebrate their eccentricity and be dedicated to fulfilling their own potential. So, while there is so much pressure to collapse into a couple, a perfect partner also takes responsibility for being a guardian of the other's individuality. Because before a person can be faithful to another, they must first have found a way to be a trusty companion to their true selves. This delightful dichotomy can be overlooked in the desperate need to defend ourselves against the despair of loneliness.

"If a man is not faithful to his own individuality, he cannot be loyal to anything." ~ Claude McKay

This quote confirms what you may have heard before, that you can't give to others what you first don't have for yourself. If you do not know and love your own sexuality, in all of its complexity and contrasts, then you cannot provide this sense of compassion for anyone else.

"You can only love another to the extent of your insecurities." ~ Belinda Tobin

Core Concepts

A person's level of maturity has a direct impact on their sexuality.

Our sexuality evolves as we progress through stages of adult development, transitioning from a reliance on external validation to a deeper sense of autonomy.

Based on Dr. Kegan's Theory of Adult Development, maturity progresses through key stages including:

- The Imperial Mind: Driven by self-interest and external rewards.
- The Socialised Mind: Defined by others' expectations and the need for validation.
- The Self-Authoring Mind: Independence, self-worth, and decision-making based on personal values.
- The Self-Transforming Mind: Embracing complexity and continual growth, free from rigid expectations.

Over half of adults operate from the Socialised Mind, conforming to societal norms, and making decisions driven by fear of rejection or desire for approval.

During the Self-Authoring stage, individuals build more balanced and authentic relationships, making decisions based on personal values rather than external pressures.

You first need to know and appreciate your own sexuality before you can effectively bring care and compassion to anybody else.

Chapter 11 – Sexuality and Morality

"My sexuality is not an inferior trait that needs to be chaperoned by emotionalism or morality." ~ Alice Bag.

Morals are a code of conduct that governs our individual behaviour and our connections with others. While morals are predominantly individual decisions, they are shaped by the society in which we live. Our parents are the first teachers of what is right and wrong, and we learn to appreciate the comfort that comes with conformance. As we grow, societal norms also have a strong hold over our behavioural choices, with very few of us courageous enough to risk bearing the title of deviant.

The Advantages of Morality

Having a set of clear behavioural standards across society has many advantages. Morality can create strong communities based on shared values and an agreed set of acceptable behaviours. Moreover, it can contribute to consistency and stability for all its citizens. A great sense of safety and security comes from knowing what to expect from those around you, and those behaviours that may cause harm to you and your family are banned.

Conforming to mainstream morals also makes each person's life easier. Individuals don't have to do the hard work of self-reflection and creating their own character[49]. They save this trouble by picking one off the shelf that society has already created for them.

It is much simpler to paint over our complex, challenging and often conflicting needs with rigid rules about what is right and wrong. By relying on simple and clear societal rules, we can defer dealing with our desires and duplicities indefinitely.

Morality's Shortcomings

For all of its benefits, morality also has its shortcomings. Firstly, severe standards repress the reality and richness of personal complexity and inhibit individuality.

"To me, the whole process of being a brush stroke in someone else's painting is a little difficult" ~ *Madonna*

The lack of diversity can also significantly disadvantage effective decision-making. As John Stuart Mill[50] acknowledges, men are imperfect creatures and cannot see all sides of the truth. Rejecting or ignoring alternative moralities also limits comprehensive considerations and risks substandard social policy.

Morality, while having the potential to bring people together under a common set of values, can also create division and disruption. Morals often focus on what a group already has in common, which is a restrictive view based on current circumstances. It is less used to spur conversations about what people would like to have in common, which creates the potential for broader, more inclusive communities. For example, holding onto the moral of monogamy makes polygamists different and thus dangerous. However, what if the focus instead was on the mutual desire to create and sustain loving and respectful relationships? A less granular view of morality may allow meeting on common ground and advancing actions that benefit a much wider proportion of the population.

Additionally, morality has the potential to create more trauma than it prevents.

"If trauma is untransformable experience, then any moral belief — that is simply abided by rather than personally transformed is akin to trauma."[51]

When a person is not free to consider how the moral fits within their system of values and how it may contribute to or constrict their flourishing, they are prevented from making this moral their own. It will sit as a rule that will always be tainted with some degree of concern and contest the individual's sense of sovereignty. Where feelings of powerlessness result, pain will soon follow.

While there are advantages to relying upon social conventions to create your character, there are also significant risks. In conversations with people on their deathbeds, it was found they held the following regrets[52]:

- Not pursuing their dreams and aspirations.
- Following the life others expected of them.

- Not expressing their feelings and speaking their mind.
- Not allowing themselves to be happy.

While numerous and complex factors may hold people back from living their best lives, blindly following social norms is one way to limit authentic self-expression and generate grief in those for whom redress is no longer possible.

Where there are rigid and unrealistic morals, there also exists a greater likelihood of a radical recoil. The instincts and desires people hold do not diminish just because there are rules against them. They find other, less public channels for expression. Perhaps this is one of the reasons for the popularity of porn. It provides a convenient way to role-play fantasies not possible in a bonded relationship, if only in people's imaginations.

"Morality has hardly made us better people; but it has certainly enriched our vices." [53]

In his thought-provoking book *Straw Dogs*, John Gray proposes another limitation to morality: It is of little value when we are caught amid conflicting needs.

"Morality is a sickness peculiar to humans, the good life is a refinement of the virtues of animals. Arising from our animal natures, ethics needs no ground; but it runs aground in the conflicts of our needs." [54]

And if there is one defining characteristic of sexuality, it is how it is drenched with conflicting desires. We seek stability as well as stimulation, intimacy as well as mystery, and we want to be accepted into the tribe, as well as to stand outside of it and be recognised as an individual. We want to be invaluable, but also independent. These opposing desires also mean we are caught in the conundrum of choosing between our moral foundations.

Moral idealism is also recognised as a major source of violence[55]. Adherence to moral codes can become the end to which any means may be justified. Moral idealism erodes procedural fairness, all in the name of a mandate. It can be used to dehumanise others who stray from these standards and, by seeing others as less than human, be used to justify all sorts of aggression and oppression.

The Moral Foundations

In his book *The Righteous Mind*, social psychologist Jonathan Haidt has identified six innate moral foundations formed from our evolutionary adaptive challenges. These are shown in the following table.

Figure 7 - The Moral Foundations

Moral Foundation	Adaptive Challenge	Characteristic Emotions
Liberty / oppression	Noticing and preventing dominance	Reactance and resentment
Care / harm	Protect and care for children	Compassion

Moral Foundation	Adaptive Challenge	Characteristic Emotions
Fairness / cheating	Reap benefits of two-way partnerships	Anger, gratitude, guilt
Loyalty / betrayal	Form cohesive coalitions	Group pride, rage at traitors
Authority / Subversion	Forge beneficial relationships within hierarchies	Respect, fear
Sanctity / degradation	Avoid contaminants	Disgust

Interestingly, those with liberal political leanings tend to focus on the first three foundations (liberty, care and fairness). In contrast, those with conservative views apply all five to their decision-making. It was also identified that the prime drivers for libertarians are curiosity, experimentation and experience. In comparison, those on the far right are motivated predominantly by fear.

When Our Sexuality Creates a Moral Dilemma

A moral dilemma arises when:

- A person needs to make a decision.
- There are multiple courses of action to choose from.
- No matter what action is taken, some moral foundation will be compromised.

Put simply, a moral dilemma is a situation with no perfect solution. Whatever decision is made will go against one of your values. In this way, there is no logical or rational methodology for resolving this dilemma. Choosing a solution will involve confusion, uncertainty and compromise. You will need to select one of the moral foundations, and sacrifice the others, and there are always consequences to your choice which are troubling.

Between Liberty and Loyalty

Because there are so many morals related to sexuality, there are also innumerable dilemmas that can result from our needs and wants. However, most boil down to the inherent conflict between the desire for liberty and the pull towards loyalty. This loyalty could be to a partner, a culture, a tradition or our parents.

"The most difficult people to be unfaithful to are one's parents." ~ Adam Phillips

For example, acting on your desire to connect with the same sex can, within certain cultural contexts, bring loads of shame onto yourself and your family. So, you are stuck between being true to yourself (in secret) or living freely in fear of your parents' reaction. There is no right choice; both have serious consequences for all relationships.

Similar is the decision to make your sexual connections monogamous. If your partner has this as a pivotal value, but you don't, then you have the choice to either comply to please your partner or contest the expectation and potentially destroy the connection. Suppose the first action is chosen, and monogamy becomes a relationship condition. In that case, you are imbuing the relationship with the foundations of fairness, loyalty to the partnership and respect for the monogamous tradition. However, simultaneously, you will have chosen against the foundations of liberty and potentially care for individual needs. In this way, the initial expectation of monogamy in the couple has already created tension. The couple can celebrate the choice made but forget that one day, the foundation of liberty they forewent may come back to haunt them with all of the ferocious resentment of an oppressed ghoul.

"Unexpressed emotions will never die. They are buried alive and will come forth later in uglier ways." ~ Sigmund Freud

The fluctuations between moral priorities may take minutes or months. Still, there will inevitably be movement between the possible preferences of liberty or loyalty.

It is a wonderful idea to think that we could all be free to ignore social conventions and satisfy our individual sexualities. However, as we have seen in the discussion around maturity, life is not that simple when you are in the Socialised Mind.

The Consequences of Moral Conflict

The above examples have shown how sexuality can create significant internal conflicts. Battles can erupt between the pursuit of personal liberty, the care for individual desires, and loyalty to our partners, parents and tradition. Our conscience can feel like it is in the centre of a civil war. So, how do we bring peace to the inner struggle that our sexuality may bring? How do we create a treaty that will quell the turmoil?

For those who are stuck in a moral dilemma due to their sexuality, they would be experiencing internal conflict and discomfort. There is a disconnect between how they are living and what they value and a contradiction between their behaviour and beliefs. The professional term for this internal conflict is cognitive dissonance. Our brains do not cope well with inconsistency. So, it is expected that the dispute will deliver many difficult emotions, such as:

- Anxiety
- Regret
- Sadness
- Shame
- Stress.

"As Freud famously remarked, the patient's symptoms are his sexual life."[56]

People can also tend to delegate responsibility for their predicament, blaming their partner, their parents, the government, or God for their stressful situation. Moreover, suppose a person feels like they don't fit within society's moral code. In that case, they can also become disoriented, confused, insecure, mistrust themselves and their feelings, and, sadly, come to believe that they are faulty or broken in some way.

Our brains are very adept at moving us away from pain and towards pleasure, so whether we are conscious of it or not, when we experience these uncomfortable feelings, we will take action to remedy the discomfort. The extensive research on cognitive dissonance tells us that we will close the gap between our values and behaviours by either:

- Changing our values to fit our behaviour (loyalty) or
- Changing our behaviour to fit our values (liberty).

If our greatest fear is loss of status or spouse, then the moral foundation of loyalty or authority is likely to yell the loudest. In this case, we will convince ourselves that the conventional standards around sexuality are correct and reinforce this value by seeking support for this view. We could also change our behaviour to remove ourselves from the temptation to act on alternative attractions and sacrifice:

"sacrifice sexual pleasure in the service of psychic survival"[57].

We choose the lesser evil of sublimation over the greater evil of loneliness. In the words of Brené Brown, it could also be argued that we choose conformity and comfort over courage.

Alternatively, suppose we are passionate about exploring our potential and crave curiosity. In that case, the moral foundation of freedom will speak more strongly. In this case, we may turn away from the moral codes of the mainstream. We will move away from relationships and role models that restrict our liberty and explore and experiment with many different forms of connection to discover more about ourselves and our sexuality.

However, where a sexual moral dilemma exists, logic is rarely successful at resolving it. This is when emotion steps back in. But because our emotions have been repressed during the period of rational reasoning, they tend to come back stronger. Emotional reactions to the disconnect between lifestyle and values can be even more powerful, increasing effects such as depression and anxiety and potentially leading to post-traumatic stress disorder[58].

Converting Conflict into Compassion

There is some good news in all of this, and that is that conflict can be a facilitator of change and growth. If (or when) the above moral dilemmas develop, they could be used to spark awareness and insight and start conversations that enable the individuals and the relationship to flourish. There are three preconditions for this to be possible, though, including:

Awareness of the conflict in the first place. With around 90 per cent of our thoughts and feelings being subconscious and around 60 per cent of adults operating from the Socialised Mind, it is likely that the person may not even be aware of the nature of the internal struggles around their sexuality. Moreover, due to a lack of clear sexuality models, it may be difficult to identify the element of their sexuality that is creating the conflict.

Insight into the impacts of the conflict. The inner turmoil may significantly affect a person's mood, attitude and relationships. The internal conflict may be spilling out into external interactions, lessening the ability to communicate about the struggles effectively.

A relationship based on care, curiosity and respect. The person experiencing the dilemma must be able to treat themselves with care and self-compassion. If they discuss this conflict with others, it must be in a space that is free from judgment. This requires two individuals who are willing to park their egos at the door and find the courage to overcome their fears about what the other person's sexuality means for them and to be there solely for support and not selfishness.

So often, though, what is going on for another person is always shadowed by concerns about what it means for us. If we are being driven by the fears of loss, loneliness and lack of self-worth, then engaging empathetically and transforming moral conflict into compassion and growth will be very difficult. Nevertheless, there is an antidote to fear, and that is love. If we can bring true love into our relationships, then we can create spaces to resolve sexuality's moral dilemmas peacefully.

One would expect that as we mature, we experience fewer moral dilemmas, as our sense of self-worth is no longer found in other people's standards but in our unique and authentic sexuality. Nevertheless, we all need to be on the lookout for where our sexuality rubs against societal moral standards for one very important reason—to alert us to the potential for shame to arise.

Core Concepts

Morality is a set of principles and rules that guides our conduct. Individual morals are shaped by upbringing and societal norms.

Shared moral standards create community stability and predictability but reduce the need for individual self-reflection and growth.

Rigid morality can suppress individuality and diversity, leading to narrow and naïve decision-making..

Sexuality often causes moral dilemmas, with personal desires clashing against societal expectations.

Moral conflict can lead to cognitive dissonance, triggering a person to change their values or their behaviour to remove the source of tension.

Moral dilemmas can spark self-awareness and growth when approached with care and curiosity.

Identifying where personal sexuality clashes with societal morals helps understand and address any sources of shame that arise in this mis-alignment.

Chapter 12 – Sexuality and Shame

The dictionary definitions of shame deal largely with the loss of esteem or standing that results from a specific belief or behaviour. We all have an innate desire to be perceived as attractive and valuable, so in this way, shame serves effective tool to maintain social order. For in the tribal days, if we did something that was "shameful", we would be ostracised. Expulsion from the tribe would surely lead to death, either at the hands of starvation, dehydration or from predators. People did not want to be pushed out of the safety of the tribe, and so shame was an internal trigger that made people painfully aware of their failures to meet social or personal standards, thus promoting conformity to group norms.

In many ways, shame has historically functioned to enforce social norms around sexuality. Society has long placed rigid expectations on what a person's sexuality should comprise and how it should be expressed, dictating what is acceptable and what is not. Shame has been used as a tool to maintain these norms, pressuring individuals to conform to conventional sexual roles or moral standards. People have been made to feel ashamed for all elements of their Sexual Self, including their physical form, gender identity and sexual desires. While men have been shamed for not being able to make sufficient or quality sexual connections, women have been shamed for making too many, being labelled as a slut.

In this way, shame and sexuality seem to be close travelling companions.

The Cruel Consequences

Brené Brown goes further to define shame as:

"The intensely painful feeling or experience of believing that we are flawed and therefore unworthy of love and belonging—something we've experienced, done, or failed to do makes us unworthy of connection."

So, shame is much more than losing respect or regard for ourselves or those around us. It has us believing that we are fundamentally bad people and unworthy of health or happiness.

Shame in sexuality works to strike fear into one of our most basic human needs—the need for connection. Because sexuality is such a personal and vulnerable aspect of our identities, shame hits at the very core of who we are. It can cause us to hide, withdraw, or deny our sexual selves, often leading to a range of unhelpful responses. These can include:

Withdrawal – Shame can make people retreat into themselves, avoiding intimacy, connection, or even discussion about their sexual needs or desires. This can lead to feelings of isolation and depression.

Avoidance – Some may avoid confronting their feelings of shame by numbing themselves to their sexual desires or by denying their sexual identity altogether. This self-protective behaviour keeps them from addressing the root of their shame.

Attacking the Self – Internalised shame can manifest as self-destructive behaviour, such as self-criticism or engaging in harmful sexual activities in an attempt to punish oneself.

Attacking Others – In some cases, sexual shame may lead to lashing out at others, manifesting in frustration, anger, or a desire to belittle or control others' sexual expressions to protect one's own damaged sense of worth.

Figure 8 - The Reactions to Shame

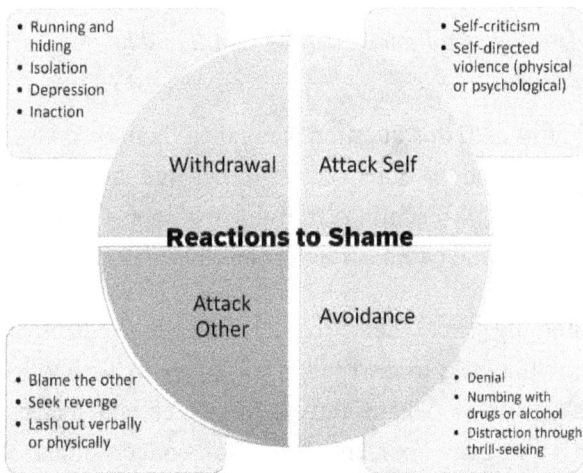

None of these responses allow for healing or healthy sexual expression, and they often drive individuals further away from understanding and accepting their sexuality.

The following diagram shows two different scenarios, the first being where shame is responded to by attacking others, and the second where it leads to withdrawal. In both cases, shame has resulted in a cycle of destructive behaviour, with shame becoming further internalised and entrenched and resulting in a greater separation from self and others.

Breaking the Shame Cycle

To heal sexual shame, we must first acknowledge its presence and understand how it manifests in our thoughts and behaviours.

To do this, you can ask yourself one simple question.

Do I believe I am worthy of health and happiness?

If the answer to this question is no, then there is some shame that you need to uncover, acknowledge and neutralise. Otherwise, it will continue to dwell within and direct you to take actions that cause suffering for yourself and others.

Overcoming sexual shame requires support, self-compassion, and a willingness to rewrite the narratives we've internalised about ourselves. Shame thrives in silence and secrecy, but when we open ourselves up to conversations about sexuality—free from judgment and fear—we allow for healing and growth. Shame doesn't need to be a life sentence; it can be the starting point for deeper self-awareness and more meaningful connections.

Shame triggers a sense of worthlessness

Shame

To defend against the internal pain, the person withdraws physically and/or psychologically.

Sadness

Depression about the person's inability to "fit in" or form connections.

Withdrawal

Immediate relief.

Relief

The person loses the opportunity to build courage and confidence in their own sexuality. Further encounters only add to the sense of awkwardness.

Limited growth

Reinforced beliefs about worthlessness and inability to form constructive connections.

Reinforced beliefs

Shame triggers a sense of worthlessness

Shame

To defend against the internal pain, feelings are converted to anger and blaming others.

Anger

Lashing out at other or self either physically or psychologically.

Violence

Immediate relief.

Relief

Reflection followed by further shame and feelings of helplessness.

More shame

Reinforced beliefs about worthlessness and inability to form constructive connections.

Reinforced beliefs

Core Concepts

Shame acts as a social tool, historically enforcing conformity to sexual norms by creating fear of ostracism and rejection from the tribe.

Sexual shame can target physical form, gender identity, and sexual desires, affecting both men and women differently (e.g., men for inadequate connections, women for making too many).

Brené Brown defines shame as the painful belief of being flawed and unworthy of love and belonging.

Common responses to sexual shame include withdrawal, avoidance, self-criticism, destructive behaviour, or lashing out at others.

Shame often leads to cycles of harmful behaviour, reinforcing internalised feelings of worthlessness and deepening disconnection.

Healing sexual shame requires self-compassion, empathy, and open, judgment-free discussions.

Breaking the shame cycle begins with self-reflection, asking: "Do I believe I am worthy of health and happiness?"

If the answer to this question is no, then shame may be driving behaviours that cause suffering to yourself and others.

Chapter 13 – How Porn Dumbs Down our Sexuality

Our innate sexuality is intelligent, imaginative, inspirational and invincible. Despite all attempts to subdue it and destroy it, it still exists as an essential part of our being and the cornerstone of our creativity. However, just like the puritanical patriarchs before them, modern-day pornographers are doing their darndest to degrade it. Put simply, pornography is dumb. Sure, it has its place in the process of arousal. Still, fundamentally, it is a force that breeds stupidity and cowardly silence. Porn is dumb because of the absurd and perverse effects it has on the viewers, the silence it imposes on the rights of women and children and its subjugation of the inherent beauty of human sexuality. The stupidity that porn is breeding does not bode well for the people who watch it, the creation of meaningful connections, or for human evolution.

What is Pornography?

First, it is important to get on the same page about what we mean by pornography. The technical definition of pornography is:

Materials produced principally for the purposes of sexual arousal.[59]

This definition sounds completely harmless, and if this is your understanding of pornography, you may wonder what I am making such a fuss about. Just in case you are still living in the seventies, though, pornography has evolved in a deeply disturbing way from the bare-chested beauties gracing the centrefolds of Playboy. It was only a matter of time before these images were normalised, and the viewers became desensitised. The result? The pornography industry has to up its game and seek more extreme thrills to get and keep its viewer's attention.

There are now two genres of porn that have incredibly dangerous effects:

1. Gozo porn
2. Pseudo-child pornography (PCP)

Gonzo Porn

Gonzo porn is what some people may know as hardcore. It depicts women being debased, dehumanised and physically tortured. And don't think that access is restricted to such sexual violence. With a simple Google search, your children can view women being treated as sexual slaves, with no regard for their physical or emotional wellbeing. In fact, viewers are lured in on the promise that they will see these sluts get what they deserve. Just one search and one click, and your children are in a world of justified cruelty — brutality that becomes linked with sexual pleasure. With one simple search, I was confronted with images of women being fisted, ejaculated upon and having every orifice penetrated at once.

Pseudo-child pornography (PCP)

PCP treads a line very close to child pornography. While it uses women over the legal age of 18, they are dressed like toddlers or young girls and are surrounded by toys and other childhood artifacts. They are usually found holding dolls or teddy bears, sucking on lollypops and looking shy. PCP promises the viewer that during this video, they will get to see this innocent young thing become the whore we all know she is. While there is always the argument that the girls shown in these films are adults, there is no doubt that PCP depicts and normalises children as attractive sexual partners.

Let's Define Dumb

For such a small word, dumb really socks a punch. Calling someone or something dumb tramples on two intense sources of pride — the ability to think well and express our thoughts and opinions.

Being dumb means you are incapable of either. Merriam-Webster defines the word as follows[60]:

Showing a lack of intelligence.
Requiring no intelligence.
STUPID
Lacking the human power of speech.
Temporarily unable to speak.
SILENT

Porn Makes People Stupid

I would be very worried if I were the first to say this. Thank goodness, though, there is a raft of psychiatrists and neurosciences that have been professing this fact for years, so I don't need to bear the brunt of initial controversy. The research on the damaging effects of porn on the brain is clear and conclusive, and this is backed by thousands of heartbreaking testimonies from those who have lost years of their lives in a dull, stupefied land of porn addiction.

Put simply, porn does not include any of the complex cues and realistic rewards that come with the human connection. It is usually watched in isolation and relies only on the touch of a button. It does not take a great amount of creativity, intellect or effort to get a pleasure hit. On the other hand, we have seen in the Sexuality Circle that human connections include a complex mix of physical and chemical cues, touch, talk and emotional exchange. There is a high level of intelligence required to interact with another being, and none of this is captured in the world of repetitive role plays that are modern pornography. The result is that those who watch porn lose the ability to understand others and succeed in real relationships.

The Senseless Side Effects of Porn

"Isn't it ironic." ~ Alanis Morrisette

Ironically, many people turn to porn as the source of education about how to be sexually intimate and yet end up being less confident, less connected, and more alone as a result.

It is also ironic to learn that two of the nasty side effects of watching too much porn are decreased libido and erectile dysfunction. That's right, porn kills sexual performance. This is due to the chemical and functional changes that occur in the brain from being exposed to the unnatural highs that porn presents.

Tolerance Lowers Libido

In the world of porn, variety, shock, and surprise are just one tap away. In just one click there is a new conquest, a new position, new punishments — the novelty is endless. The pleasure experienced releases huge amounts of dopamine, and with each click, the intensity continues. Like any other drug, over time, a point of tolerance is reached, and the feel-good reaction a person once got from watching porn subsides. This compels the person to watch more and more extreme porn to get the same pleasure kick. No longer is the person aroused by the same sexual adventures they once were. Not only does the sex drive wane, but this paves a path to porn addiction. Alarmingly, the research also shows that accessing pseudo-child pornography (PCP) increases the demand for real child pornography and provides men with both a blueprint and stimulus to undertaking child sexual abuse[61].

The Natural Is No Longer Is Good Enough

The fact is that a real person can never live up to the continual thrill that is presented with porn. Lovers look dull compared to the perfectly sculpted porn mistresses, and the desires of a normal human being pale to the limitless and extreme situations that the porn actors put themselves in. When a brain has become used to the high thrill of porn sex, anything real no longer becomes stimulating. The result is that a person can no longer get aroused with a lover — men can't get it up, and women can't get wet. The sexual dysfunction created by porn can take months to resolve. It also creates a vicious cycle as people feel broken, ashamed, unworthy and withdraw even more. People become dissatisfied with their intimate relationships and distressed when they cannot satisfy their lovers.

Again, it is ironic that people may first turn to porn to "spice up" their sex life but end up with it being destroyed altogether.

Any entertainment that delivers the exact opposite of its promises is a stupid proposition. Don't just take my word for it, though; head into the NoFap community to hear from those people (Fapstronauts) who are leading much brighter lives after moving away from porn.

Porn Is Not Just Entertainment

Sure, you can argue that porn was never meant to be intelligent. It is there purely for light relief from the pressures of life, a stimulus to brighten dull days and a bit of entertainment to satisfy our primal brains. I would agree with you if it weren't for the fact that porn has no longer become entertainment. It has become the source of sex education for our children.

The average teenager encounters porn at around 11 years old[62]. Most adolescents will have viewed pornography, with around 93 per cent of boys and 62 per cent of girls regularly exposed to pornographic images[63]. You may think that our children should distinguish between the fantasy that porn portrays and the reality of healthy sexual relations. Unfortunately, you would be wrong. Around 44 per cent of males and 29 per cent of females report wanting to act out what they see in porn[64]. Three-quarters of young women say that pornography increases pressure on girls to act a certain way and increases their level of insecurity in intimate relationships[65]. Around 70 per cent of teenage boys admit that pornography has had a damaging impact on their view of sex and relationships[66].

"I believe we are experiencing a seismic cultural shift, as our global, shared sexual culture moves from the erotic to the pornographic. This move, from an erotic culture to a pornographic culture, is deeply damaging. We are losing the depth of emotion, joy, connection and extreme pleasure that our ancestors knew lay at the fundamental heart of the human sexual experience. The eroticism of the previous ages, which had so much to say about shared pleasure, is being lost to the technologic, sanitisation of the commerce of sex." ~ Fern Riddell[67]

Porn's role in sex education has severe and negative consequences. Research reveals that this consumption strengthens harmful gender stereotypes and increases the perpetration of sexual aggression and tolerance of receiving it. It fills our children's minds with lies about sexual relations. For example, it creates the impression that women are always up for sex and are always willing to do what a man wants, regardless of how painful, harmful or humiliating it may be[68]. While parents and educators may desire to create an environment of gender equality and respect, porn is much louder than the positive messages. We all know that it is generally the loudest voice that wins.

Porn use is now so prevalent that until the rise of the NoFap community, researchers found it impossible to find a control group for their studies. There were just no young adult males who were not exposed to it regularly. Porn has become the norm.

Porn is a Form of Puritanism

I'm sure if I suggested to a porn master that he was a Puritan, he would laugh in my face (both mockingly and dramatically, I suspect) and suggest I was crazy to think his sexual adventures could be equated to religion in any form. Of course, we think of Puritans as religious zealots, largely because of their role in condemning the liberties introduced by the Church of England. But let's take the more generalised definition, where a puritan is:

"One who practices or preaches a more rigorous or professedly purer moral code than that which prevails."[69]

You may argue that porn is free from morality or go further to claim that the violence it portrays against women is the antithesis of virtue. And you would be right. However, suppose you consider a moral code simply a standard of behaviour. In that case, porn expounds a moral code in every single movie. With each viewing, it preaches that it is right and just for women to be submissive, and it is justified and righteous for men to use and abuse women for pleasure.

But how is the moral code porn portraying purer than societal norms? Simple. Because the scenarios that play out in porn are free from anything that vitiates the primal power of men. There is no resistance, no challenge to the brutality, and no suggestion that the women involved may have desires of their own. Instead, victims of the violence display pleasure or do not react at all. The porn masters have stripped away anything that may weaken the sick story of satisfied submission they are selling. And if what you are peddling is poison, then the purity does not make it better; it just makes it more deadly.

The excruciating reality for women is that the pure moral code advocated in porn does become deadly. The National Plan to End Violence Against Women and Children[70] admits that pornography reinforces stereotyped sexual attitudes and contributes to harmful sexual behaviours. Pornography normalises brutality, oppression and possession, all of which are precursors to domestic violence.

Puritans also must maintain control. Why? Because they are scared shitless about what will happen to their power if they don't. We see this evidenced in every porn film. But what if the female porn actors were permitted to break the script and play the scene as they would like? What would happen if they started to reject the orthodox acts of buggery, ridicule the dogma of dominance, or refuse the sodomy and suppression that is at the core of porn plots? A loss of control over the female players would be the end of porn as we know it, and so discipline and submission of the female must prevail.

Porn Is a Product of Patriarchal Fear

Porn, then, is a product of patriarchal fear - fear of the largely unknown and unexplored female sexuality. Fear of losing power and not being able to perform if the tables are turned. You see, this is where men are at a distinct disadvantage. They have a very obvious display of sexual virility, and so it must be a constant fear for many that they will be publicly shamed by a limp dick. By controlling the narrative, and the situation, they can maintain power through their penis.

And so, it is this sexual stereotype and incompetent relationship role modelling that our youth are learning. In this way, the porn puritans are incredibly successful at distributing the doctrine of dread, debasement and denial of feminine sexuality. They are proficient at mass pussification.

Porn Proliferates Cowardly Silence

"Silence is golden but when it threatens your freedom it is yellow.[71]" ~ Edmund Burke

A decade ago, there were already 12 acts of violence per scene in the top porn films. It is easy to understand that this number is likely to have escalated in recent years. The porn masters are well aware of the science behind desensitization and know that to keep their viewers hooked, they need to continually add surprise and shock to the playlist. What this means is that porn is becoming increasingly more violent and cruel. Gonzo porn has become almost mainstream, with images easily sourced of women being debased and dehumanised. This is not entertainment; it is sanctioned torture.

The most dangerous thing found in these films, though, was that there was no resistance to the abuse. Instead, victims of the violence displayed pleasure or responded neutrally to the cruelty[72]. Silence is porn's response to violence against women and children.

The silence that porn imposes on the rights of women and children threatens their freedom by normalising sexual violence and suggesting that silence is the correct response. In this way, the silence that the porn stars portray in response to the violence is a direct affront to the freedom of the most vulnerable in our society.

In her forthright and shocking book *Pornland*[73], Gail Dines makes a wonderful point. We would never allow these practices in the public domain if they were conducted based on race or religion. We would not permit images of torture, restraint, physical violence, and degradation to African-Americans or Jews. So why the hell are we allowing these images of women to be freely circulated without reprimand?

Porn also threatens the freedom of all people to express their sexuality in a way that is meaningful for them. With porn becoming the norm and the default sex education for our children, we are becoming programmed to think that the scenarios and behaviours of the actors are what human sexuality is all about. But as we have heard, humans are complex, emotional beings, and our bodies, brains, and spirits are unique and beautiful. By seeing only superficial physical gratification, we are silencing the wonder that is human sexuality, and this is to the detriment of deep connection, creativity and the conscious evolution of the entire human race.

"There is no dignity with the human dimension is eliminated from the person. In short, the problem with pornography is not that it shows too much of the person, but that it shows far too little." ~ Pope John Paul II

Porn Prevents Human Evolution

Evolution is defined as:

A process of continuous change from a lower, simpler, or worse to a higher, more complex, or better state.

GROWTH[74]

Everything that we have just heard about porn proves that it is not a tool for human evolution. It is keeping us simple, preventing the flourishing of human relationships, and impeding the understanding of our full human sexuality. Moreover, it works to continue the suppression of women and facilitate violence toward children, which is maintaining a cruel status quo. Porn does nothing to help humans move to a higher or better state of existence. It is not doing anything to assist us in understanding our full potential, growing, and bringing love and compassion into the world. It is destroying lives and families and so has caused much more harm than pleasure or entertainment.

Perhaps the only benefit that porn has provided is by providing a clear example of what we are not. Our modern generations are shocked and appalled at the terror created by the Nazi regime, and yet within Germany at the time, it was not only accepted but supported. Similarly, the Iraqi invasion seemed justified in 2003. Now, many Americans feel deep regret for the pain and suffering that the eight-year war created. In my naïve optimism, I can only hope that the world is slowly waking up to the cruel consequences that porn has for individuals and our society. I truly hope that this is the beginning of one hard lesson learned and that the outcome is greater intelligence and support for those previously silenced.

Wouldn't it be wonderful to have our boys and men thinking about the types of sex and relationships they want and not be prejudiced by porn propaganda? Wouldn't it be delightful if our girls and women permitted themselves to explore their sexuality and define their ideal relationships without the influence of patriarchal puritanism? Wouldn't it be a revolution if we all began thinking for ourselves instead of letting the loud voice of fear and violence scare us away from progressing towards our potential?

Core Concepts

Pornography reduces sexuality to a superficial, simplistic transaction, damaging the complexity and beauty of human sexuality.

Pornography, especially genres like Gonzo porn and pseudo-child pornography (PCP), dehumanises women and normalises sexual violence and exploitation.

Porn's impact leads to lowered libido, erectile dysfunction, and addiction, desensitising individuals to natural sexual experiences.

Watching porn often makes real-life human connections less satisfying, causing a disconnect from healthy, intimate relationships.

Porn serves as an inadequate and harmful form of sex education, especially for youth, shaping unrealistic expectations about sex and relationships.

Pornography perpetuates patriarchal control, maintaining dominance over women and suppressing female sexuality.

Pornography prevents human evolution by stalling emotional, intellectual, and spiritual growth, keeping people trapped in simplistic, harmful understandings of sex.

Chapter 14 – Sexuality Through the Lens Of The Natural Laws

We have seen how our sexuality is influenced by so many aspects, both within our bodies and from the social context in which we live. However, even if we think we are civilised creatures, we cannot escape the fact that we are children of the earth affected by the rhythms of our world. That is why I think it is invaluable to inspect our sexuality through the lens of the immutable principles that work within and around us— what are known as the natural, Hermetic, or Universal Laws.

The Universal Laws

The seven Hermetic Laws were named after their creator, Hermes Trismegistus, who was revered as a god of wisdom in the first century AD. They are said to govern the operation of every living being, our planet, and the universe. While they were considered both blasphemous and heretical at the time, centuries later, they became vital inputs to the transformational philosophies of the Renaissance. Nowadays, these laws are entrenched in the plethora of self-development teachings covering attraction, manifestation, and self-mastery. If you were to look closely at the celebrated teachings of Tony Robinson, Zig Ziglar, Eckhardt Tolle, Deepak Chopra and even the Dalai Lama, you would see how they are built upon these universal laws. Even our modern-day psychological systems draw from aspects of these inescapable truths.

1. Mentalism — The All is mind; The universe is mental.

2. Correspondence — As above, so below; As below, so above. As within, so without; As without, so within.

3. Vibration — Nothing rests; Everything moves; Everything vibrates.

4. Polarity — Everything has poles; Everything has its pair of opposites; Opposites are identical in nature but different in degree.

5. Rhythm — The pendulum swing manifests in everything; The measure of the swing to the right is the measure of the swing to the left.

6. Cause and effect — Every cause has its effect; Every effect has its cause.

7. Gender — Gender is in everything; Everything has its masculine and feminine principles. Gender manifests on all planes.

The theory is that functioning in alliance with these laws brings peace, wisdom, and prosperity. Operating in ignorance and opposition to these principles brings tension and turmoil. So, it is interesting to investigate how well our beliefs about our sexuality and our behaviours follow these laws or where we are acting out of alignment with these natural ordinances.

The Universe is Mental- Sexuality is a Mental Construct

"There is nothing either good or bad but thinking makes it so." ~ William Shakespeare

The principle of mentalism tells us that our own conscious and subconscious thoughts shape our experiences of this world. Our truths are merely mental constructs. So, while we might associate our sexuality with our bodies, in reality, it is a manifestation of our mind. As we have seen, there are so many social constructs around sexuality, but what is good or bad, right or wrong, cool or crass, are merely thoughts. Mentalism tells us that because our minds create our reality, we can change our view of things and, in doing so, change our circumstances and outcomes. Simply put, if your sexuality challenges you, then you just need to think differently about it. The law of mentalism also behoves us to care for the invisible and spiritual aspects of our lives, as these are the precursors to our physical wellbeing and prosperity.

The law of mentalism also provides advice for Sexual Connections. Our worlds are shaped by processes within our innermost recesses. It takes great awareness and insight to comprehend these and their complex influence on our lives. If it is a journey to understand our own selves, then it is nearly impossible to know anyone else fully. It is ludicrous to think we can understand everything going on in another person's mind or heart. What you are told or see is only a fraction of the content of their intricate inner world. Changes in behaviour, needs or desires are not necessarily "out of character"; they are just different components crawling out of the crevices of their subconscious. We are all complex creatures, and there is a whole world beneath the surface of our awareness that needs to be acknowledged.

As Above, So Below - Your Reality is based on Your Beliefs.

"The outer conditions of a person's life will always be found to reflect their inner beliefs." ~ James Allen

The principle of correspondence builds upon that of mentalism by enlivening the nexus between our mental states and current circumstances. It describes how the quality of our lives depends on the quality of our thoughts and that changing our life trajectory also requires a change in our beliefs. This principle is embedded in and illustrated by the modern Cognitive Behavioural Therapy (CBT) model shown in the following diagram.

The CBT model shows the process by which our beliefs become self-fulfilling prophecies. Our beliefs begin a whole chain of thoughts, feelings, and actions, the outcome of which is then used to confirm or contest the beliefs that beget them. Sometimes, it is easier to see how this all works through an example. So here is one I prepared earlier!

Figure 9 - The Cognitive Behavioural Therapy Model

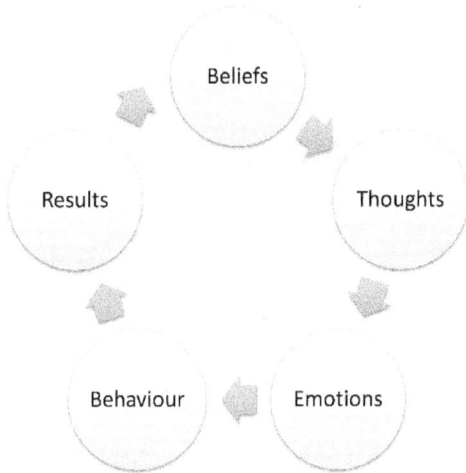

Example 1: Sexuality is Constant

Suppose you have been heterosexual all of your life thus far. Then you begin to become attracted to people of the same sex and even desire to be close to them. If you believe that sexuality is static, then this sequence of thoughts and events could occur.

Belief: I AM heterosexual.

Thoughts: This attraction to others of the same sex is weird and wrong.

Feelings: Fear, guilt and possibly shame.

Behaviour: Internalising the issue, withdrawal or lashing out at your partner from frustration.

Results: The attraction to the same sex continues with a sense of great conflict. It may cause ruptures in existing relationships and also have the person coming to believe they are faulty in some way.

Example 2: Sexuality is Fluid

Let's see how merely changing the beliefs about sexuality can create a completely different and possibly more compassionate pathway.

Belief: I am an ever-evolving sexual being.

Thoughts: This attraction to others of the same sex is interesting, and I think I should explore it further.

Feelings: Curiosity.

Behaviour: Open and non-judgemental internal investigations and possibly supportive conversations with a partner.

Results: A deeper understanding of the self and appreciation of the person's contrasts and complexities. Potential experimentation and evaluation of connections with the same sex. These reinforce the belief that the person is capable of change and that this can be supported in a compassionate and constructive way.

As these simple and somewhat idealistic examples illustrate, the beliefs we hold around our sexuality ignite a string of explosive expectations and reinforcing behaviours. Put simply, your beliefs about sexuality will create your experience of it. These expectations do not have to be grounded in reality, as made clear by Gabriel Marcel:

"In themselves, facts have no authority."[75]

That beliefs are the driver of our Sexual Selves and the constructs that determine the success of our connections is both enlightening and challenging. Because we largely work from subjective and subconscious beliefs, we must be willing to dig into ourselves to understand our sexuality. We must also dedicate ourselves to constructive communication to share this with any sexual partners.

The principle of correspondence also explains the theory that we cannot give understanding and compassion to others unless we first have it for ourselves. Without self-awareness or dedication to self-development, we will struggle with our own sexuality and sexual connections with others. Issues of trust, faith, and freedom begin in the hearts of individuals and flow out into all of our relationships. In this way, the law of correspondence empowers us to resolve all conflicts by looking firstly at the struggles within ourselves.

Nothing Rests – Change is Inevitable

"Change is inevitable. Growth is optional." ~ John C. Maxwell

The law of vibration corresponds to the Buddhist law of impermanence and is an inconvenient truth for those who have a desperate need for stability. This principle reminds us that change is natural and that nothing stays constant. At a physical level, we change each day dramatically, with 330 billion cells being replaced daily. This state of flux is no different in our intangible mental and emotional worlds and is also apparent in our connections with others.

As stated by James Hillman, the quest for constancy in commitment is a delusion:

"Such an arrangement can't hold because life wants to break in on that deathly demand for absolute stability."[76]

Not only do external forces want to shake things up continually, but our bodies are also made to modify our relationships. We have seen how, within ourselves, hormones and their fluctuations play a huge role in our health and many elements of our Sexual Self. They also impact our Sexual Connections in surprising ways.

Evolutionary anthropologist Helen Fisher[77] reports that the heady hormones that drive romance (dopamine, norepinephrine and PEA) endure in our systems for only a few years. This period corresponds nicely to the timeframe required to achieve reproduction and care for an infant. The biological support may keep the couple together long enough to procreate and ensure the survival of their offspring.

However, George Bernard Shaw did not need science to tell him that the passion felt at the beginning of a romance is only temporal. His lived experience and observation of others led him to this conclusion well before hormone research was rife:

"When two people are under the influence of the most violent, most insane, most delusive, and most transient of passions, they are required to swear that they will remain in that excited, abnormal, and exhausting condition continuously until death do them part."

After these heady hormones of romance decline, the prime chemical driver of behaviour is oxytocin, known best for feelings of compassion, contentment, and connection. The intoxicating effects of new love dwindle physically, to be replaced by the less exciting, although integral components of a deep and meaningful relationship.

Interestingly, oxytocin is also a hormone that facilitates increased self-awareness and openness to new experiences. This suggests that after the waning of the original romance, it may be a prime opportunity to use the pair bond as a foundation for a new wave of personal growth.

This story's moral is that sexual fluidity is not just a scientific concept but is captured within the natural world. Our sexuality is, like every other natural phenomenon, inconsistent and changeable. Similarly, how you feel about an intimate partner is bound to change over time, and your partner will inevitably experience changed feelings for you. In addition, what you seek from a relationship can shift. Some may remain wedded to the thrill of novelty and naughty. In contrast, others may move on to be comforted by routine and predictability. This natural evolution of relationships is the fundamental recognition in the no-fault divorce system. There is no longer the expectation that a couple will live up to the promise that "till death do we part." It is well known that even if the couple stays together physically, they can detach emotionally and spiritually. While all started bright and rosy, over time, beliefs, thoughts and emotions can alter to a point where there become "irreconcilable differences".

The question, then, is not one of whether the nature of our Sexual Self or Sexual Connections will change; it is how we will react when they do. As suggested by John C. Maxwell, it is the reactions to the changes that occur which are important. In clinging to false beliefs, social conventions, unrealistic expectations or a desire to get back to how things used to be, we can miss the opportunity for personal learning and growth that is embedded in every change. This law then presents us with a significant opportunity: the continuous ability to develop, grow and expand as individuals. It also provides the power to create connections with enough space to cater for the movement of each individual and the flexibility that will allow each person to flourish.

"No matter who you are, no matter what you did, no matter where you've come from, you can always change, become a better version of yourself." – Madonna

Everything Has Its Pair of Opposites – Opposites Always Exist

Everything in existence has an opposite and dwells within this dichotomy. It is impossible for anything to exist in the absence of its antithesis. You cannot know what joy is until you have known sadness. You cannot know hard until you know soft, hot until you have known cold, and you cannot know what war is unless you know peace. In the same way, as stated by Adam Phillips:

> *"Monogamy comes with infidelity built in, if only as a possibility."*[78]

The challenge polarity holds then for our sexuality is to recognise that whatever form our sexuality currently takes, its opposite also exists. Wherever there is masculine energy, the feminine is also there, maybe just in the background. Wherever there is attraction to the opposite sex, an attraction to the same sex still exists as a possibility. Wherever there is a desire for slow, seductive sex, there is also the potential need for a passionate pounding. And while now there may be courage and exploration, it is foreseeable that at some time, there will also be insecurity and isolation. This law celebrates our dichotomies and tells us that our contrasts and internal conflicts are not to be seen as challenges but are to be celebrated as an enactment of universal energies.

Where this may create difficulties, however, is when we expect a sexual connection to meet all of our opposing needs. Humans are complex creatures, and while we may crave spontaneous stimulation and sensual surprise, we also have an innate need for safety and security and to feel comfortable and confident in the arms of our companions. We seek absolute intimacy, wanting to know and be known by another completely. Still, we also need uncertainty and novelty to drive attraction. We want a working partner for the dirty domestic chores as well as the seductive satisfier of our sexual desires. We yearn for connection but also desire autonomy. We seek the excitement of lust but also the contentment of love. Humans are one big conundrum of contradictions. The law of polarity tells us that this is not a problem; it is natural. We get stuck when we demand one person to fulfil all of these roles.

In the past, we would have been in a tribe or community that would have delivered a range of people and various experiences; our modern, insular lives mean that,

"Today, we turn to one person to provide what an entire village once did."[79]

While modern romance promises that you can get all these conflicting needs met in one place, Esther Perel, an expert in relationship counselling, responds by stating, "I'm not convinced"[80]. Other experts further declare this expectation as nothing short of an outrage that only leads to sorrow.

"Declaring that a man and a woman must meet each other's needs in all respects, at once, for their whole life, is a

monstrosity that necessarily gives rise to hypocrisy, hostility and unhappiness."[81]

The irony is that placing such great dependence on one person does not create more stability, but in fact, the opposite; it makes us more vulnerable. The entirety of our self-image and our physical and emotional wellbeing is vested in a person who, we have seen, is also an inherently complex web of illogicality and inconsistency.

One could also assert that it is completely selfish and downright disrespectful to expect one person to satisfy the entire scope of our divergent needs. It places enormous pressure on someone else to be your "everything". While we tend to expect that our partner will meet all these opposing expectations, we are quick to exclaim that they are unrealistic if they propose we should do the same for them. Such is the "hypocrisy of the conjugal life"[82].

For many, the existence of opposites creates confusion and conflict. However, what is missed is the energy created between them. Each holds a different degree of the same energy, and the swing between them creates an exciting dance. This energy is lost when the push is for settling at one point, trying to be the same and seeking stability. When we seek unity of identity, or melding with our mate, the result, as suggested by Thomas Moore, is the squashing of our unique individual spirit:

"Whenever I hear someone insisting on unity, in whatever context, I worry about the suppression of the soul, which is

many-sided and full of the richness and the tension of multiple urges. "[83]

The law of polarity presents significant opportunities for understanding and loving our sexuality. Being aware that opposites exist within ourselves and may erupt at any time enables us to exist with greater freedom, not fearing change or conflict but treating it with care and compassion. Recognising that we may have opposing needs also allows us to find multiple sources to fulfil them, reducing the pressure on one person to be your everything and burdening those we say with love with unrealistic expectations.

The Pendulum Swing Manifests in Everything – We Are All Swingers

"Everything old is new again."

The principle of polarity tells us that there are opposites in everything. The principle of rhythm then tells us that there is a continual movement between the contrasts. The pendulum perfectly presents this principle, showing that there is movement between opposites and that the extent of the swing over to one side determines how far the swing is over to the other.

We see this principle in action from a macro perspective in society. Repression swings to emancipation, spiritual mystery shifts to a reliance on scientific truths, organisational design moves from formal hierarchy to freelance networks, and governments sway from left to right and back again.

What does this mean for our sexuality? Well, it depends on how extreme you play. Pegging the pendulum of your sexuality at any extreme will only result in equally extreme behaviour but in the opposite direction to what you had hoped to achieve. The further your expectations are away from the natural equilibrium point of balance between the opposing forces, the more you set yourself up for the potential of an equal and opposite backlash.

For example, suppose you spend your days sexualising yourself to be deemed attractive, admired and accepted. In that case, it is just as likely that you will also have periods of deep depression and loneliness as well. Being pegged at the pure, prudish end of the sexuality scale can, over time, result in a radical and rebellious swing to promiscuity and pornography. This law tends to explain why often 'Catholic girls' are deemed the most sexually available – they are swinging to the opposite of what they are told is right and true.

"I wouldn't have turned out the way I was if I didn't have all those old-fashioned values to rebel against." ~ Madonna

The principle of rhythm makes it clear that our needs swing between the poles over time. We can move radically and rapidly from feelings of great selflessness to a drive for selfishness and self-satisfaction. Sometimes, we can shift in seconds from the intense pull towards security and stability to a burning desire to run wild and free and seek all of life's adventures. In this fast-moving world of competing perspectives, it is easy to feel dazed and confused and wonder, "What is wrong with me? Everyone else seems to have figured out what they want; why can't I?" You don't see the internal fluctuations also occurring within those who seem to have their act together.

Sometimes, though, it can take years for the pendulum to swing from feelings of satisfaction to its opposite or from the comfort of conventional sexual connections to a craving for something revolutionary. When this pivot does occur, it can also cause deep introspection and self-criticism. It can cause a person to question whether they will ever be satisfied or if they are broken or faulty in some way.

Fundamentally, this principle tells us that we will always go through various opposing emotions and thoughts and that we are not single-dimensional beings. Everything is alternating all the time. Just as waves come and go, it is natural for feelings of love and lust to ebb and flow, rise and fall. For this reason, it should not be a surprise when we feel conflicted in our relationships or see "unusual" behaviour from our partners.

Perhaps this principle can be best summed up by saying, "we are all naturally swingers"!

The fluctuations predicted by the law of rhythm can put great pressure on our sense of identity and the Sexual Connections we may cling to as a source of stability. However, with awareness and compassion, we can use this principle to our advantage and to strengthen, not shrink, our understanding of our sexuality, for there is no doubt that oscillations will occur. The most important thing is what follows the fluctuations. Do we try and restrain the natural flow of life and attempt to secure it in position, clinging to the rope to hold it in place? If this is our chosen response, we should also be prepared to end up with rope burn.

Or is it possible to create a sexuality that celebrates both firmness and fluidity? For example, aligning expectations, boundaries and behaviours close to our natural human states can minimise tension and reduce the likelihood of backlash. Knowing that it is natural for our feelings to fluctuate, we can lessen shock and conflict when they occur and invite greater empathy and compassion for ourselves and our partners. In this way, the rhythm principle empowers us to allow all of our emotions to dance together and create an exclusive and authentic cadence.

Every Cause Has An Effect- Garbage In, Garbage Out

The law of cause and effect tells us that every situation we encounter has a source, and every action we take has a consequence. This proposition may seem simplistic, but its implications are immense. For example, your decision that same-sex relationships are indecent is no random occurrence but a result of many internal and external contributors. You may like to think of it as an independent and considered decision, whereas it is more likely to be based on a complex set of preceding conditions.

Likewise, the depth of understanding about our sexuality is dependent upon the quality of our self-exploration and introspection. Self-awareness does not spring forth like magic; it is made from meaningful reflections, investigations and seeking insights about our inner nature. Similarly, the success of our Sexual Connections depends on the quality of inputs – understanding, compassion and love, instead of judgment, control and fear. The law of cause and effect delivers a real opportunity via the virtues of self-awareness and honesty. Being truthful with ourselves and being open to finding the lessons in past failures creates a foundation for ongoing confidence in and comfort with our sexuality. Entering Sexual Connections with this same integrity and intention also bodes well for relationships supporting evolution and growth. Suppose a part of your life feels like garbage right now. In that case, this law calls on you to investigate the inputs you are investing into it, and question whether they are of the quality you need. Are you giving sufficient time, energy and attention to deliver the optimal outcomes?

Everything Has Its Masculine and Feminine – Balancing Gender Energy

The final principle of gender builds upon the principle of polarity. It refers specifically to the gender energy element within the model of sexuality. This law states that opposing feminine and masculine energies reside in everything, and the interplay of these is the source of vitality and creativity. This principle does not suggest that people identifying as male are only comprised of masculine energy and that those with a gender identity of female espouse only feminine energy. Instead, it is professed that both masculine and feminine energy resides in all things. The ultimate aim is to have both energies working together to ignite life.

The masculine energy is assertive, progressive, and explorative, creating drive and motivation. It is an energy of logic and loves order, solutions, and plans. It gives direction and instruction. The opposing feminine energy gives care and nurturing. In contrast to the logical progression of the male, feminine energy is fluidity in motion. Instead of prioritising solutions, feminine energy places the greatest importance on relationships.

In balance, the masculine and feminine dance beautifully together, fostering energy that creates life. However, it is easy for these energies to get out of balance. When there is too much masculine energy, everything feels like work. There is always a problem to be solved, and the focus is always on the destination instead of being able to enjoy the journey. The outcome of extreme masculinity is feelings of being overwhelmed and exhausted. Without the proper balance of the feminine, it feels like a lot of action is happening but with very little outcome. People can feel lost and question why they began this adventure in the first place.

However, when there is too much feminine energy, there can be flightiness and a lack of focus. Without the structure and order of the masculine, people can feel like they are being blown around by the wind and at the whim of external circumstances. There is a preoccupation with maintaining relationships but an accompanying lack of focus on an end goal or purpose. This imbalance is akin to flitting around, enjoying all the sights but forgetting about organising a place to spend the night.

There is no doubt our modern lives are masculine-heavy. Our days are filled with making plans, following rules and solving problems. We are driven by science and logic, with little room for spirituality and intuition. We are so busy operating in the world of work that there is very little time for nurturing and investments in all of our connections, especially the one with ourselves. Even within a couple, it is likely that both partners are working towards the egalitarian model, where there are opportunities for financial and personal growth open to both parties and equal sharing of power. However, instead of true equality, where both the masculine and feminine energies can ebb and flow, and each partner is free to express both, the reality is that we end up with both partners operating from the masculine energy. It is no wonder, then, that our relationships end up feeling draining and devoid of purpose – and we have already seen what this state does to our sexual desire and vitality.

Sustained vitality is a function of a swing between opposites and the forces that draw them to each other. Our sexuality then requires a balance of gender energies, both within our own lives and in our interactions with others. We also need to create a space to be vulnerable and safe enough to express each energy. It is relatively easy to take some time out for ourselves from this frantic world for a bit of self-care for our whole being, and more specifically, our Sexual Self. But it takes much more considerable insight and courage in Sexual

Connections to negotiate roles for each partner around the masculine and feminine energies, yet this is required to keep the relationship alive.

Egalitarianism and equality are noble pursuits, but if not engaged with the wisdom provided by the principle of gender, it could be a death knell for the satisfaction and survival of any relationship. The opportunity for Sexual Connections then becomes creating a relationship model where both energies can flow freely, where there is room for both achievements of ambition and attention to affiliations, and which sustains attraction and desire instead of dampening them.

"Join the male and the female and you will find that what is sought." ~ Maria Prophetess

---

The Profound Potential of the Principles

The natural laws provide a great deal of intelligence about how we can enable our Sexual Self and our Sexual Connections to thrive. Simply, we need to:

Understand that our beliefs shape our reality and work to unearth the harmful or flawed beliefs that may be holding us back from living fully and freely.

Ensure we are using great information, including our individual insights, authentic truths, and lessons gained from growth experiments, to help shape decisions about our sexuality.

Treat change and conflict with compassion. Our complexity and the swing between sides of our nature may create surprises, but when treated with care, they can be a great source of knowledge.

Make time for the masculine and feminine energies. The vital force that is our sexuality will shrink without the waters of both.

You may choose not to believe these laws and remain convinced that these principles are not immutable but idiotic.

"The half-wise, recognising the comparative unreality of the universe, imagine that they may defy its laws. Such are vain and presumptuous fools, and they are broken against the rocks and torn asunder by the elements by reason of their folly." ~ *The Kybalion*[84]

However, these principles are in play whether you believe in them or not. The real choice becomes whether you will see them as insurmountable challenges and shun them from your considerations around sexuality or employ them as opportunities to strengthen your Sexual Self and Sexual Connections.

These laws provide a foundation on which we can ground all of our relationships in reality and have truthful, open and critical conversations about the way things really work. These laws empower each individual to create a sexuality that aligns with the natural flow of life rather than one that fights against them. Life and relationships are hard enough in themselves; why would you choose to embed additional conflict?

Core Concepts

The seven Hermetic or Universal Laws govern all life, including our sexuality.

Mentalism: Our sexuality is shaped by our mental constructs.

Correspondence: Our internal beliefs reflect in our external experiences.

Vibration: Change is constant.

Polarity: Opposites exist within everything.

Rhythm: Everything moves between extremes.

Cause and Effect: Our experiences and the quality of our sexual relationships are shaped by the inputs we invest.

Gender: Balancing masculine and feminine energies, fosters vitality and sustained desire.

Aligning with these natural laws enables a more authentic, dynamic, and fulfilling sexuality while resisting them creates tension and struggle.

Chapter 15 – Is Your Sexuality Driven By Love or Fear?

As we have seen in the Cognitive Behavioural Therapy Model, emotions are the immediate precursor to action, pushing us towards certain behaviours. Often there is a view that there are "bad" or "good" emotions, with this delineation being made based on how the emotions make you feel. Those that feel pleasant and uplifting, such as happiness, joy and love, are classified as good emotions. While those such as anger, disgust, shame and sadness are classified as "bad". In reality, though, all emotions are messengers. When we are willing to listen, our emotions can provide valuable insights, enhancing our confidence in our authentic sexuality.

The Five Primary Emotions

According to Jim Dethmer, there are five primary emotions, each conveying specific messages:

Anger: Indicates that something is no longer beneficial and requires change, whether it is outdated beliefs, behaviours, or relationships. It calls for establishing or reinforcing boundaries and the capacity to say "no" without justification.

Fear: Signals that something important needs to be faced or learned. It encourages full presence and awareness, prompting attention to new skills or behaviours that need to be acquired.

Sadness: Reflects the need to let go of something significant that is departing. It urges acceptance of reality and the release of roles, dreams, behaviours, or relationships that no longer serve us.

Happiness: Suggests that something or someone should be celebrated or appreciated. It calls for taking the time to acknowledge personal achievements or positive experiences, fostering a sense of internal wellbeing.

Sexual Feelings: These feelings indicate a time for new ideas, creativity, and innovation. They encourage building upon these ideas and taking action to create something unique.

As discussed previously, many people take the sexual urges they feel at face value, believing that they are being driven to act on their desires by physically connecting with another. However, as this analysis shows us, sexual feelings may be calling us instead to create something, to fuel and foster our creative spirit and bring something to life that is unique to us.

The Levels of Consciousness

Dr David Hawkins has undertaken a deeper dive into emotions, using Applied Kinesiology to analyse the energy signals of numerous emotional states. The result is his Levels of Consciousness Model, which is shown on the following page.

In this model, emotions traditionally seen as bad, such as shame, guilt, fear, and anger, are categorised as emotions of Force. These emotions exert pressure, influencing behaviours by causing inaction or demanding excessive effort. They constrain individuals, creating a sense of obligation and burden, and often lead to a feeling of being out of control of one's life and destiny. This is why, historically, such emotions have been classified as "bad" - because they take away our sense of agency.

Figure 10 - The Levels of Consciousness Model by Dr David Hawkins

Levels of Consciousness by Dr David Hawkins

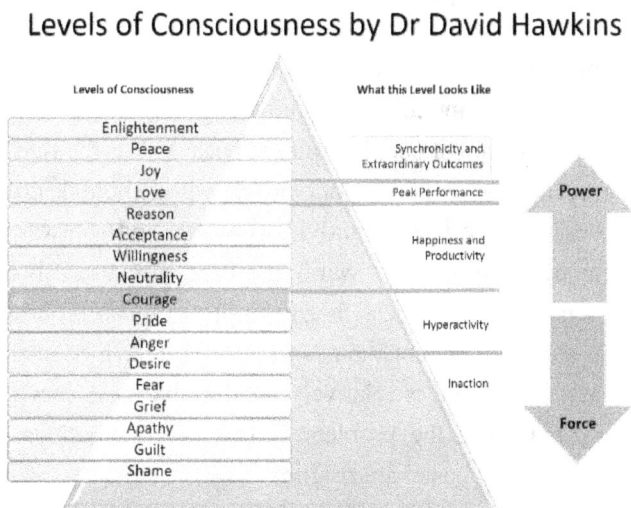

Conversely, there are emotions or states of being that draw upon intrinsic strength, allowing individuals to live authentically and to learn and grow. These are known as emotions of Power and include love, joy, and peace. These emotions feel good because they draw from our internal strength and push us towards our highest potential.

While Force emotions may appear undesirable compared to Power emotions, Dr. Hawkins suggests that experiencing lower-level emotions is part of a necessary journey through various states of consciousness. These emotions offer insights into personal and universal dynamics, motivating one to progress toward higher levels of consciousness characterised by love and joy. Individuals can gain the motivation and skills needed to seek freedom and fulfilment only by experiencing the constraints of emotions like shame, guilt, and fear. And so, while we have discussed the destructive nature of shame, this model shows that with support, it is possible to move away from it to more positive states of being.

Some may wonder why pride is categorised as a force emotion in this model. It is acknowledged by Dr Hawkins that it is the level most people aspire to because it is the first level that feels good. All the emotions below pride hold destructive power and reflect negativity inward and outward. In comparison, pride feels warm and fuzzy because it is based on some sort of success. For example, you can be proud of your achievements or the possessions you have been able to amass. Because it is relatively comfortable, it is easy to get stuck here, but the problem is that the foundations upon which pride is based are fragile.

Pride is based on external circumstances, for example, the value of your property or others' positive opinions of you. Pride, then, is not a solid and sustainable source of positivity. Due to the inevitable law of impermanence, sooner or later, things will change, and you may be back down at fear, grief, guilt or shame all over again. Interestingly, pride is also an emotion correlated directly with discrimination in all its forms. It is used to puff oneself up at the expense of others who are believed to be less worthy than yourself.

One thing that must be highlighted in Dr. Hawkins' model is the central role of courage in transitioning from Force emotions to Power emotions, acting as a bridge between these two states. Throughout this book, we have repeatedly discussed courage as a necessary condition for authentic sexuality and compassionate connections. Here, we also see it as a precursor to becoming the highest and happiest version of yourself. This emphasis on courage empowers and motivates individuals to embark on their journey towards emotional growth and self-fulfilment.

There are so many emotional states that influence our sexuality, but there are two that warrant much further investigation. These are the opposing energies of love and fear.

Love and Fear Are Opposites

The natural laws tell us that there must be an opposite to the concept of love. Most would say it is the obvious answer - hate, but some wise people have suggested that the opposite of love is actually fear. I wish I could remember who told me this so I can thank them for this insight. It has helped me understand so much of what I see in this world. More importantly, it has given me a simple and powerful way to reflect on my motivations. I only need to stop and ask myself:

"Am I doing this out of love or fear?"

The earliest reference I can find for the assertion that love and fear are opposites comes from Seneca the Younger (4BC - 65AD). He said:

"True love can fear no-one."

This statement suggests that there can be no fear when true love is present, and the opposite, where there is fear, true love is an impossibility. Here, we see the certain proposition that love and fear are opposites and cannot exist together. This view confirms my assertion that:

"You can only love someone to the extent of your insecurities."

With further research, I found that this assertion was made by two amazing modern and open-hearted thinkers – Elisabeth Kubler-Ross and John Lennon.

Elisabeth Kubler-Ross was a revolutionary in how we care for the dying and how we deal with death. She certainly would have seen the extreme perspectives of those facing their last days and the family and friends who were preparing themselves for a life without their loved ones. Here's what Elisabeth said:

"There is only love or fear, for we cannot feel these two emotions together, at exactly the same time. They're opposites. If we're in fear, we are not in a place of love. When we're in a place of love, we cannot be in a place of fear." ~ Elisabeth Kubler-Ross

John Lennon was one of history's greatest poets, philosophers and protagonists. During his days with the Beatles, he passionately professed that "all you need is love" (1967). His solo song 'Imagine' (1971) was a testament to his vision of a world founded upon love, where there is no fear, and all the people are "living a life of peace". John has been recorded as saying:

"There are two basic motivating forces: fear and love." ~ John Lennon

So why is this important? Why should we care about which one, love or fear, we are motivated by? Why is it important to know which one is driving our decisions regarding our sexuality? To answer this question, let's look at the outcomes of each scenario.

What Does Acting From Love Look Like?

First, let's define love. In this context, I am not talking about the ecstatic sexual highs, eros, or the rousing obsession that is romance. Here, I define love not as a feeling but as an action.

"Love is the action taken to bring happiness, reduce suffering and help another achieve their highest potential."
~ Belinda Tobin

Therefore, love is not just what you give to other people but also what you do for yourself. It is not an emotion but a way of being in this world. Acting from love is about being motivated by deep and honest care for your wellbeing, spirit, and future self and care for the world around you. It means being vulnerable enough to show your true self and brave enough to commit to something bigger than yourself.

Looking at the descriptions provided by Kubler-Ross and Lennon, it appears that when you act from a place of love, you will see a flow of positive emotions. The person acting from love will feel happiness, contentment, peace and joy. Moreover, they will share this peace and joy with all around them. Lennon believed that acting from a place of love was vital to authentic creativity. He saw that when you are working from love, you are open to life's reality but have the passion and excitement to contribute and bring positive change. These views are very similar to the work done by Dr David Hawkins in exploring the levels of consciousness, where the level of love is associated with peak performance. It appears then that operating from a perspective of love is beneficial not only for the person undertaking the activity but also for the good of the connections they make and the communities they are serving.

What Does Acting From Fear Look Like?

Fear is the opposite of love, so it understandably produces negative emotions, insecurity, and inaction. These emotions are rooted in the prime concern for what others think of us rather than being true to ourselves. When we act from fear, we hand our power over to others and allow them to define our sense of self-worth. It appears that living in the Socialised Mind means that we are continually challenged by the force of fear.

Spending our days in fear is nothing short of destructive – for the person living in fear and the world around them. Because as Lennon so wisely perceived:

"When we are afraid, we pull back from life."

Fear closes us down to others and our potential. We mistrust ourselves and sacrifice our ability to make a positive contribution to this world. When we fear how others react, we do not give all of ourselves. We are not honestly and fully ourselves. The result is that we live in a state of conflict – there is a war between who we know we truly are and that which we display to others. Care, creativity and contribution are stifled. Gandhi recognised this when he said:

"Fear kills the soul."

unique and full life.

"Poor is the man whose pleasures depend on the permission of another." – Madonna

2. **We are afraid of what we could be**. Inherently, each one of us knows what we are capable of. It is grand, beautiful and brave. And yet, it is risky to shine. What would happen if I released what is within and lived a big and bold life? What would happen if I loved myself enough to let myself live freely and fully in this world? This deep fear of succeeding, of our power, is captured succinctly by Marianne Williamson:

"Our deepest fear is not that we are inadequate. Our deepest fear is that we are powerful beyond measure. It is our light, not our darkness, that most frightens us".

210

Similar to the intergenerational trauma that exists around masturbation, I suspect we are all carrying scars from our ancestors around our sexuality. Especially those who have come from strict religious traditions, we have been taught to fear our sexuality as a form of evil, as something that will harm us and hurt others. Our parents, grandparents and generations past have been told to suppress their sexuality, to sublimate it, and to show it was sinful. The moral boundaries steeped in fear stopped many from seeking to understand it, so we are left with the legacy of lost opportunities and corrupted comprehensions.

Nevertheless, we also have an innate wisdom that weaves through each generation, and which may have been guarded tightly in the past, is still available to us here in the present. We are now blessed with societies that have swung more to the moral foundations of care and liberty than to loyalty to strict and senseless conventions. In this context, then, we have a chance to carry on the work that the brave and bold of the past began and build a new future founded on love for our children. We can help heal the horrors experienced by our elders and enable the next generations to bring love into their lives, their communities and to this earth.

How Do You Move From Fear To Love?

This world is geared to keeping us in a state of fear in so many ways. Our legal and educational systems are founded upon punishments and penalties. Marketers rely on FOMO to keep us spending our money on status symbols and scare us with the view that signs of ageing are not attractive. Politicians regularly claim catastrophic consequences that will arise from opposition policies. So, in this context, how do you move from a place of fear where your awesome spirit and sexuality are stifled to a life of freedom and authenticity? How do you begin operating from a place of care for yourself and your true wellbeing? There is one initial step: finding the courage to understand and accept yourself. But how the hell do you become courageous?

If you look the word courage up in the dictionary, you will see that the definition of courage is:

"The ability to do something that frightens one."[85]

This definition holds the key to what courage is all about. Courage does not mean that you don't feel afraid. In fact, it is the exact opposite. Fear is an inherent part. Without fear, bravery does not exist. Dr Hawkins confirms this in his Map of Consciousness, asserting that one must work through the 'Force' emotions before rising above and operating from power. I remember reading an interview with Paul McCartney when he discussed the insecurity that John Lennon had about how we would remember him. Despite this concern, Lennon kept going. He kept pushing the boundaries and expressing himself in and outside his music.

This is because courage is choosing to move beyond fear. It is the choice to sit with the discomfort of the unknown because of something more important.

"Courage is not the absence of fear, but rather the assessment that something else is more important than fear."
~ Franklin D. Roosevelt

Courage is about making the decision that being true to the amazing energy that is your sexuality is more important than allowing fear to keep you stuck in conformity. It is about deciding that stepping into your power is more valuable than giving in to your anxiety.

But more than just coming from a cognitive exercise, courage comes from action.

It is about trying new activities, meeting new people, finding those things that bring you joy and bliss, fuelling your passions, and making your heart sing.

As this definition suggests, courage is not a quality endowed at birth or something our Fairy Godmother gives us with a wave of a wand. It is an ability, a skill that is developed over time and with dedicated practice.

Courage Is a Skill

So, courage is not just something you are granted. Like reading, driving a car or playing an instrument, it is a skill you learn over time. You will be pleased to know that thanks to enormous research undertaken into how people learn, there is a clear set of steps to take to build your courage muscle. Dr Russ Harris outlines these steps in his model called The Confidence Cycle[86]:

Figure 11 - The Confidence Cycle

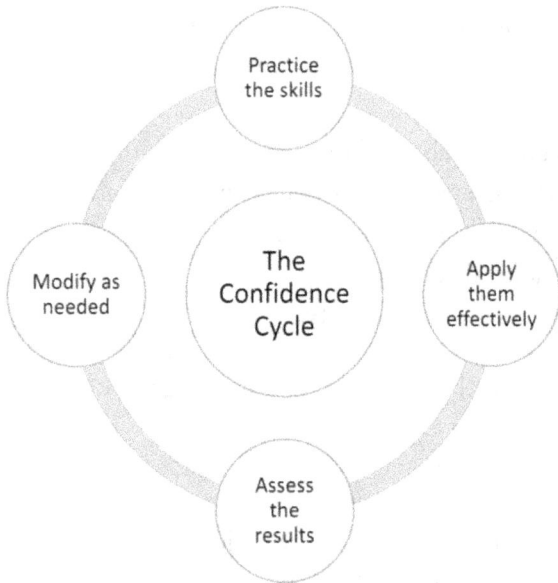

Working through these steps will build confidence in whatever new endeavour you embark upon. More than this, though, engaging the Confidence Cycle in your daily life will build faith and trust in yourself that you can learn new things, change, and grow into the person you truly want to be.

The Sexuality Skills

So, what skills do you need to be practising to build confidence in your sexuality? I would suggest that these are the skills of:

Self-awareness and introspection – to learn what feels right for you and under what circumstances you feel challenged or threatened.

Self-investigation – understanding your beliefs, how they impact your life, and how you respond when they are contested.

Self-Intimacy – to understand what brings you pleasure and to create a beautiful connection with your own body.

Self-compassion – to recognise when you are suffering, how you may be contributing to your own discomfort, and to support yourself in taking the actions necessary to reduce it.

Assertive communication – to find strength in your own voice, ask for what you want, and build constructive connections based on your truth.

Sexual health – learning to understand your unique rhythms and how to care well for your body.

Safe exploration – where and how you like to explore your boundaries and sexual preferences.

Not taking yourself too seriously – we can tend to become so serious about our sexuality that it becomes just another thing we have to succeed at. Yes, you can take the pursuit of your potential incredibly professionally, but don't lose the ability to laugh at yourself along the way.

Establishing a support network – to help you learn and grow from your experiences.

Let's use an example to help us see how the Confidence Cycle works in reality – how about the indomitable Madonna? Madonna signed her first record deal over forty years ago, in

1982. Since then, she has continued pushing the boundaries of her identity and music. Some may say she has continually reinvented herself, but she has a different take on things:

"I am not reinventing myself. I am going through the layers and revealing myself." ~ Madonna

She admits she is plagued with insecurities but still dedicates herself to her craft. She is driven by her value of artistic integrity. She is continually seeking to understand her sexuality and is bold and brave enough to provide a role model for others to do the same. Moreover, Madonna understands that while such pursuits are serious, a sense of humour is essential.

"I laugh at myself. I don't take myself completely seriously. I think that's another quality that people have to hold on to... you have to laugh, especially at yourself."

Madonna knows how transient popularity can be, but has swung with the opposites, and allowed it to create new pathways and newfound freedoms instead of damaging her identity.

"I've been popular and unpopular successful and unsuccessful loved and loathed and I know how meaningless it all is. Therefore, I feel free to take whatever risks I want." ~ Madonna

The Madonna we know and love was not born fearless, but somewhere along the way, she chose love for herself. She chose to step out of the room of fear, beyond her insecurities, and into the room of love, which has inspired so many.

"And as we let our own light shine, we unconsciously give other people permission to do the same. As we are liberated from our own fear, our presence automatically liberates others." ~ Marianne Williamson

Calling On Your Courage

It takes bravery to start doing things you love and do them in a way that resonates and supports your spirit. It takes guts to go deep and understand your sexuality and bucket loads of bravery to share that with other people. It takes a great deal of nerve to question why things are done a certain way and decide that you will do things differently. It takes even more valour to take action to help your spirit shine and make the biggest and best contribution you can make in this world.

While it may come naturally to act from love, it takes a great deal of courage to love yourself. And yet, loving yourself, in all your glory, your spirituality and your sexuality, is the most courageous thing you may ever do.

This world has enough fear, and it is creating so much suffering. We need your courage and your acts of love!

"'Cause we're only here to love
Like there's no tomorrow
So let's live each moment like
Our time is only borrowed."
~ Madonna - Borrowed Time

Core Concepts

Emotions drive our behaviours.

All emotions are messengers, calling us to grow in some way. Sexual feelings can be a call to explore and express our creativity.

Dr. David Hawkins' model shows that there are emotional states that force us downwards (such as shame, fear and anger) and those that empower us to fulfil our greatest potential (such as courage, acceptance, love, joy and peace).

Love leads to positive emotions and creativity, while fear restricts and causes insecurity.

Love is action; those that reduce suffering and a person reach their full potential.

Fear-based sexuality often stems from societal pressure or inherited beliefs, leading to suppression and conflict.

Courage is essential for transitioning from fear to love and becoming our authentic selves.

Courage is a skill developed over time, essential for living authentically and building confidence in your sexual identity.

The sexuality skills that require practice include self-awareness, introspection, self-compassion, assertive communication, safe exploration, not taking yourself too seriously and establishing a support network.

Conclusion

Sexuality is often seen as a taboo or a mystery - something to show off or be ashamed of. Yet, it's also one of the most personal and powerful aspects of who we are. As we've explored throughout this book, our sexuality goes far beyond mere physical attraction or desire—it's deeply intertwined with our creativity, spirituality, and sense of self. From the moment we're born, our sexuality begins to shape how we understand ourselves, connect with others, and contribute to the world. As Alice Walker suggests, it's even a path to enlightenment, offering profound self-knowledge if we're willing to embrace it.

We've seen how people across history have feared and sought to suppress and control this incredible force. Centuries of moral codes, societal rules, and misguided teachings have made many wary of wanting to explore and understand our sexuality. But at its core, sexuality is a power—a life-giving energy that, when understood and embraced, can bring joy, creativity, and deeper connection. It's not something to be survived, as Adam Phillips argued, but something to help us thrive.

In writing this book, I wanted to address that disconnect—the gap between what we've been told about our sexuality and what we know deep down to be true. I've spent years reflecting on my own journey, questioning the boxes I've been expected to fit into, and I realised how much I'd missed out on by not exploring my own sexual identity sooner.

Through this exploration, I've come to see that sexuality is not just about physical pleasure or reproduction. It's a sacred part of who we are, a source of wisdom, creativity, and connection. And as we age, our relationship with our sexuality doesn't fade—it simply evolves. We are always changing, and our sexuality changes with us.

And as I reflect on what we've covered, from the beauty of our physical form, the influence of shame and morality to the power of love, one truth remains clear: your sexuality is yours to define, nurture, and celebrate. Whether you're seeking greater self-awareness, deeper connections with others or spiritual enlightenment, understanding your sexuality is an essential part of that journey.

Now, as we conclude, I encourage you to continue the adventure of self-discovery. I understand that the process of uncovering sometimes previously unseen and potentially uncomfortable layers of ourselves can be difficult. There may be fears, doubts, or societal pressures that you will have to navigate. But remember, your sexuality is not something to be hidden, feared, or controlled by others. It's an essential part of your true self—a source of power, creativity, and connection that can guide you toward a life lived with more love and less fear, less unhealthy behaviours and more happiness, less shame and more ecstasy.

For you deserve a life full of love, health and happiness.

References

[1] Phillips, A. (2022). *Attention Seeking*. Picador Paper.

[2] Sigmund Freud, as quoted in Phillips, A. (2021). *On Wanting to Change*. Penguin.

[3] Jung, C. (2014). Modern man in search of a soul. In Routledge eBooks. https://doi.org/10.4324/9780203991701

[4] *Defining sexual health*. (2022). World Health Organization. https://www.who.int/teams/sexual-and-reproductive-health-and-research/key-areas-of-work/sexual-health/defining-sexual-health

[5] *Defining sexual health*. (2022). World Health Organization. https://www.who.int/teams/sexual-and-reproductive-health-and-research/key-areas-of-work/sexual-health/defining-sexual-health

[6] Graeber, D., & Wengrow, D. (2021). *The dawn of everything: A New History of Humanity*. Penguin UK.

[7] Solomon, A. H. (2020). Taking Sexy Back: How to Own Your Sexuality and Create the Relationships You Want. New Harbinger Publications.

[8] Deida, D. (2017). The way of the superior man (20th Anniversary Edition). Sounds True.

[9] Cooke, L. (2022). *Bitch: On the Female of the Species*.

[10] Dr Joan Roughgarden as Cited in Cooke, L. (2022). *Bitch: On the Female of the Species*.

[11] Cooke, L. (2022). *Bitch: On the Female of the Species*.

[12] Professor David Crews as cited in Cooke, L. (2022). *Bitch: On the Female of the Species*.

[13] Deida, D. (2017). The way of the superior man (20th Anniversary Edition). Sounds True.

[14] Deida, D. (2017). The way of the superior man (20th Anniversary Edition). Sounds True.

[15] As cited in Ridley, M. (1994). The Red Queen: Sex and the Evolution of Human Nature. Penguin UK.

[16] Ridley, M. (1994). The Red Queen: Sex and the Evolution of Human Nature. Penguin UK.

[17] Ridley, M. (1994). The Red Queen: Sex and the Evolution of Human Nature. Penguin UK.

[18] Siegel, D. J. (2016). Mind: A Journey to the Heart of Being Human (Norton Series on Interpersonal Neurobiology). W. W. Norton & Company.

[19] Ryan, C., & Jeth, C. (2011). Sex at Dawn: The Prehistoric Origins of Modern Sexuality. Scribe Publications.

[20] Moore, T. (1998). The Soul of Sex: Cultivating Life as an Act of Love. Harper.

[21] Dethmer, J., Chapman, D. Leadership. and Klemp, K., n.d. The 15 Commitments Of Conscious.

[22] Ryan, C., & Jeth, C. (2011). Sex at dawn: The Prehistoric Origins of Modern Sexuality. Scribe Publications.

[23] Staff, T. (2020, March 5). 1994: Joycelyn Elders. TIME. https://time.com/5793727/joycelyn-elders-100-women-of-the-year/

[24] Damian, R. I., Spengler, M., Sutu, A., & Roberts, B. (2018, August 16). Sixteen Going on Sixty-Six: A Longitudinal Study of Personality Stability and Change across 50 Years. https://doi.org/10.1037/pspp0000210

[25] Riddell, F. (2021). Sex: Lessons from history. Hachette UK.

[26] Frankl, V. E. (2013). Man's search for meaning: The classic tribute to hope from the Holocaust. Random House.

[27] Hegel 'A fragment on love' The philosophy of erotic love eds. Solomon, Robert C and Kathleen M. Higgins. University Press of Kansas 1991 as cited in Cleary, S. (2022). How to Be You: Simone de Beauvoir and the art of authentic living. Random House.

[28] Moore, T. (1998). The Soul of Sex: Cultivating Life as an Act of Love. Harper.

[29] Moore, T. (1998). The Soul of Sex: Cultivating Life as an Act of Love. Harper.

[30] Rosemary Reuther, as quoted in Moore, T. (1998). *The Soul of Sex: Cultivating Life as an Act of Love*. Harper.

[31] A. Van Den Broeck, B. Schreurs, K. Proost, A. Vanderstukken, M. Vansteenkiste, I want to be a billionaire: How do extrinsic and intrinsic values influence youngsters' wellbeing? Ann. Am. Acad. Pol. Soc. Sci. 682, 204–219 (2019).

[32] Macy, J., & Johnstone, C. (2022). Active Hope: How to Face the Mess We're in with Unexpected Resilience and Creative Power. New World Library.

[33] Trungpa, C. (2010). Cutting through spiritual materialism. Shambhala Publications.

[34] Tim Kasser et al., 2013. Changes in materialism, changes in psychological wellbeing: Evidence from three longitudinal studies and an intervention experiment. Motivation and Emotion. DOI 10.1007/s11031–013–9371–4

[35] Leavitt, Chelom & Dew, Jeffrey & Allsop, David & Runyan, Samuel & Hill, Edward. (2019). Relational and Sexual Costs of Materialism in Couple Relationships: An Actor–Partner Longitudinal Study. Journal of Family and Economic Issues. 40. 10.1007/s10834–019–09617–3.

[36] Rik Pieters, 2013. Bidirectional Dynamics of Materialism and Loneliness: Not Just a Vicious Cycle. Journal of Consumer Research, DOI: 10.1086/671564.

[37] Riddell, F. (2021). Sex: Lessons from history. Hachette UK.

[38] Missy Jubilee | 041 WEAPONS. (n.d.). Missy Jubilee. https://missyjubilee.com/films/041-weapons/

[39] Whyte, D. (2019). Consolations: The Solace, Nourishment and Underlying Meaning of Everyday Words. Adfo Books.

[40] Kegan, R. (1983). The Evolving Self. Amsterdam University Press.

[41] Phillips, A. (1999). Monogamy. Van Haren Publishing.

[42] Mate, G. N., Neufeld, G., & Maté, G. (2019). Hold on to Your Kids: Why Parents Need to Matter More Than Peers. Van Haren Publishing.

[43] Maslow, A. H. (1981). Motivation And Personality. Harper & Row.

[44] Mate, G. N., Neufeld, G., & Maté, G. (2019). Hold on to Your Kids: Why Parents Need to Matter More Than Peers. Van Haren Publishing.

[45] Whyte, D. (2019). Consolations: The Solace, Nourishment and Underlying Meaning of Everyday Words. Adfo Books.

[46] Greer, G. (2020). The female eunuch. HarperCollins UK.

[47] Mate, G. N., Neufeld, G., & Maté, G. (2019). Hold on to Your Kids: Why Parents Need to Matter More Than Peers. Van Haren Publishing.

[48] Mate, G. N., Neufeld, G., & Maté, G. (2019). Hold on to Your Kids: Why Parents Need to Matter More Than Peers. Van Haren Publishing.

[49] John Stuart Mill, as quoted in Phillips, A. (2021). On Wanting to Change. Penguin.

[50] Mill, J., & Benitez, P. (2017). On Liberty John Stuart Mill. Van Haren Publishing.

[51] Phillips, A. (2022). Attention Seeking. Picador Paper.

[52] The Top Five Regrets of the Dying: A Life Transformed by the Dearly Departing, Bronnie Ware, 2012, Hay House Inc.

[53] Gray, J. (2002). Straw Dogs: Thoughts on Humans and Other Animals. Granta.

[54] Gray, J. (2002). Straw Dogs: Thoughts on Humans and Other Animals. Granta.

[55] Haidt, J. (2015). The happiness hypothesis: Putting Ancient Wisdom to the Test of Modern Science. Random House.

[56] Phillips, A. (2021). On Wanting to Change. Penguin.

[57] Phillips, A. (2021). On Wanting to Change. Penguin.

[58] Hull, A.M. (2002). Neuroimaging findings in post-traumatic stress disorder. The British Journal of Psychiatry 181: 102–10.

[59] Barker, M. J. (2018). The Psychology of Sex (The Psychology of Everything) (1st ed.). Routledge.

[60] dumb. (2024). In Merriam-Webster Dictionary. https://www.merriam-webster.com/dictionary/dumb

[61] Gayle and Taylor, "Child Pornography and the Internet" as quoted in Dines, G. (2011). Portland: How Porn Has Hijacked Our Sexuality (1st ed.). Beacon Press. Page 159.

[62] Havey, A., Puccio, D., & Thomas, K. S. (2017). Sex, Likes and Social Media: Talking to Our Teens in the Digital Age. Vermilion. Page 94.

[63] Lis, L. (2020). No Shame: Real Talk With Your Kids About Sex, Self-Confidence, and Healthy Relationships. Page 151.

[64] Lis, L. (2020). No Shame: Real Talk With Your Kids About Sex, Self-Confidence, and Healthy Relationships. Page 151.

[65] Havey, A., Puccio, D., & Thomas, K. S. (2017). Sex, Likes and Social Media: Talking to Our Teens in the Digital Age. Vermilion. Page 102.

[66] Havey, A., Puccio, D., & Thomas, K. S. (2017). Sex, Likes and Social Media: Talking to Our Teens in the Digital Age. Vermilion. Page 102.

[67] Riddell, F. (2021). Sex: Lessons from history. Hachette UK.

[68] Dines, G. (2011). Pornland: How Porn Has Hijacked Our Sexuality (1st ed.). Beacon Press. Page xxxiii.

[69] puritan. (n.d.). In Merriam-Webster Dictionary. https://www.merriam-webster.com/dictionary/puritan

[70] Draft National Plan to End Violence against Women and Children 2022-2032 | engage.dss.gov.au. (n.d.). https://engage.dss.gov.au/draft-national-plan-to-end-violence-against-women-and-children-2022-2032/

[71] In Western cultures, yellow is the colour of cowardice.

[72] Bridges, A. J., Wosnitzer, R., Scharrer, E., Sun, C., & Liberman, R. (2010). Aggression and Sexual Behaviour in Best-Selling Pornography Videos: A Content Analysis Update. Violence Against Women, 16(10), 1065–1085.

[73] Dines, G. (2011). Pornland: How Porn Has Hijacked Our Sexuality (1st ed.). Beacon Press. Page 88.

[74] evolution. (2024). In Merriam-Webster Dictionary. https://www.merriam-webster.com/dictionary/evolution

[75] Marcel, G. (2017). The Mystery of Being. Andesite Press

[76] As quoted in Moore, T. (2015). A Religion of One's Own: A Guide to Creating a Personal Spirituality in a Secular World (Reprint). Avery.

[77] Fisher, H. (2017). Anatomy of Love: A Natural History of Mating, Marriage, and Why We Stray. W. W. Norton & Company.

[78] Phillips, A. (1999). Monogamy. Vintage.

[79] Perel, E. (2017). Mating in Captivity: Unlocking Erotic Intelligence (Reprint ed.). Harper Paperbacks.

[80] Perel, E. (2017). Mating in Captivity: Unlocking Erotic Intelligence (Reprint ed.). Harper Paperbacks.

[81] Barash, D. P., & Lipton, J. E. (2002). The Myth of Monogamy: Fidelity and Infidelity in Animals and People. Holt Paperbacks.

[82] Beauvoir, S. de, De Beauvoir, S., Borde, C., & Malovany-Chevallier, S. (2011). The Second Sex. Van Haren Publishing.

[83] Moore, T. (2015). A Religion of One's Own: A Guide to Creating a Personal Spirituality in a Secular World (Reprint). Avery.

[84] Initiates, T. (2018). The Kybalion: Centenary Edition. Van Haren Publishing.

[85] Dictionary.com | Meanings & Definitions of English Words. (2021). In Dictionary.com. https://www.lexico.com/definition/courage

[86] Harris, R., 2011. The Confidence Gap. Boston: Trumpeter.A

P.S.

About the author

About the Understanding Series

Read on

Find out about the next book

Meet Belinda Tobin

Belinda Tobin is a researcher, author, producer, and avid explorer of the human experience with all its challenges and complexities. Her works span fiction, non-fiction, poetry, tv series and film. However, they all share a common purpose, to foster a more conscious, compassionate and connected future.

Find out more about Belinda and her projects at www.belindatobin.com.

About the Understanding Series

"The highest form of ignorance is when you reject something you don't know anything about." — Wayne Dyer

Understanding Press was founded with a simple yet profound mission: to help each of us step into our power through knowledge and to pave the way for wise action.

The Understanding Series is the first project for Understanding Press. It provides clear and concise information about some of the most fundamental issues and pressing problems of our time. Here are the current titles in The Understanding Series.

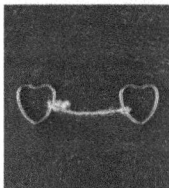

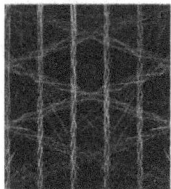

Read On

Understanding Monogamy

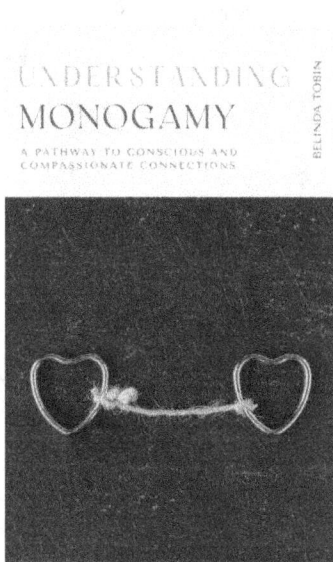

A pathway to conscious and compassionate connections.

Our intimate relationships are in a state of flux. Marriage, once considered a sacred institution, is increasingly overlooked, while divorce is a common feature of family life. Online, millions tune in to see cheaters exposed, and more people are exploring alternative arrangements like open marriages and polyamory. These trends suggest that monogamy, as traditionally practised, may no longer align with the needs of our modern, secular society—or that our current model is fundamentally flawed.

Understanding Monogamy explores the idea that while monogamy is not natural, it has become the norm, creating a moral dilemma for individuals and society. Science has shown that humans are not inherently suited for lifelong, exclusive partnerships. Yet, monogamy persists, and rejecting it without understanding its roots only replicates the conflicts it creates. This book delves into how monogamy became the default relationship model and exposes the myths that distort our expectations of it.

While societal change may continue to challenge monogamy, it remains the gold standard for many. To reduce the suffering caused by unmet expectations, Understanding Monogamy encourages readers to examine their own beliefs about love and sex and how these shape their experiences in relationships. By developing a deeper understanding of these dynamics, individuals can navigate coupledom with greater awareness and authenticity.

Understanding Monogamy is an essential guide for anyone considering a sexually exclusive relationship, struggling within one, or exploring alternatives. It provides valuable insights and practical guidance, helping readers make conscious, compassionate choices in their pursuit of love. Because everyone deserves a relationship that is true to who they are and filled with love.

Read On

Understanding Violence

"Peace cannot be kept by force; it can only be achieved by understanding." – Albert Einstein.

Understanding Violence is a heartfelt exploration born from the author's continued distress at the family and domestic violence crisis that has been continuing for decades. To solve the problem of violence, we must first fully understand it, not just one part, but its totality. This book goes beyond the headlines, delving into the varied and often hidden ways violence manifests in our society—from the overt to the subtle, from the physical to the psychological. It shows family violence as one traumatic symptom of a much larger disease. Reducing violence in society then is not just about pointing fingers at "bad people"; it's about understanding the culture that allows violence to thrive and recognising that we all play a role in its perpetuation.

Drawing from research, personal reflections, and expert insights, the author emphasises that understanding is the first crucial step toward change. By calling out violence in all its forms and unpacking the beliefs, emotions, and systemic issues that underpin violent behaviours, Understanding Violence invites readers to reflect on their own actions and the world around them. It challenges us to look honestly at how violence infiltrates our everyday lives, whether through media, politics, entertainment or unexamined attitudes.

This book is for anyone who believes in a more compassionate, peaceful world. Whether you're a policymaker, a community leader, or someone seeking to make a difference in your own life, Understanding Violence offers insights to help break the cycle of harm at the source. By fostering a deeper understanding, we can all contribute to meaningful change—starting with ourselves.

UP

UNDERSTANDING PRESS

For more titles, go to:

www.heart-led.pub/understanding-press

www.ingramcontent.com/pod-product-compliance
Lightning Source LLC
Chambersburg PA
CBHW052125270326
41930CB00012B/2757